# CHÖK'LIT

*A Confection of Girlfriends*

Joanna Lynne Krenk

Copyright © 2016 by Joanna Lynne Krenk

All rights reserved. This book or any portion thereof may not be reproduced or used in any manner whatsoever without the express written permission of the publisher, except for the use of brief quotations in a book review or scholarly journal.

First Printing: 2016

ISBN- **13:978-1523788446**
ISBN- **10:1523788445**


Cover Design: VivianElle Invitations

"Like" Joanna Lynne Krenk on Facebook
www.facebook.com/joannalynnekrenk

In memory of my first girlfriend, Deb

# CONTENTS

Introduction .................................................................7

Deb ...........................................................................11

Lisa ..........................................................................23

Sue, Sheri, & Nanette ...........................................29

Karen .......................................................................37

Debra Sue ...............................................................45

Brandy ....................................................................55

Karen C. ..................................................................61

Monica ....................................................................67

Ja & Lee ..................................................................77

Afterword ...............................................................84

A Word on Grief ....................................................86

Acknowledgments ................................................89

# Introduction

I adore my husband. He is my rock. When I waver and almost tip, he catches me and leads me to solid ground. I laugh with him, and he often laughs because of my silliness. He is serious and focused when I am flippant and scattered. I want to die first so that I don't have to live here on earth without him.

However, he is not a girlfriend. They are cut from a different cloth.

Friendships last seasons—some last long seasons and some incredibly short seasons. Currently I find myself in a season of abundance. Not too long ago, I retreated and closed up, feeling isolated and alone. I had girlfriends surrounding me, but I kept most of them at arm's length and pretended that life was tranquil. It wasn't. Now I review in my mind my girlfriends from all arenas of my life: running, church, camping, school, and lifers. I am in a season of abundance. While I am thankful to be in this season, its importance may have been lost if I hadn't trudged through my season of isolation. In that season I learned that a sister can't be replaced. Her specialness is unique. Those qualities taken for granted aren't mixed the same way in any other person. What I found, though, is that each of my girlfriends had one similar characteristic, maybe two. That could be why I was attracted to the friendship to begin with. I recognized a familiarity between my friend and sister that encouraged me to trust enough to share life in a way that resulted in a special kind of relationship: girlfriend.

While I have been and continue to be blessed by a myriad of friends, this work focuses on a span of approximately five years following my sister's death. It was a tumultuous time for me. I am sure you can imagine the roller coaster of emotions I suffered when I lost my best friend, my first friend, my big sister. I mistakenly thought I could fill the hole in my heart with someone else—maybe a lifelong friend, a sister-in-law, a trio of ladies who in my mind were one. The truth eventually was exposed, and I share that with you here, in this exploration of female friendship.

Like my favorite trail, friendships have hills that are challenging and benches overlooking tranquil lakes for peaceful times. The friends that are not acknowledged here are no less important. Friendships ebb and flow in differing lengths of seasons and with different purposes. Many friends along the way have impacted me in profound ways. I could write volumes. But I am afraid that you, dear reader, would be overwhelmed and ultimately bored silly. So to my friends not mentioned in these pages: please know that I love you, I appreciate your gifts, and if it's been too long since we talked, I miss you.

The human memory is fascinating. Two people attending the exact same event will recall different details, people, and timelines. The best example of this is the Gospels, each an eyewitness account yet not all exactly the same. Recalling the same scene, John remarks about details that Luke doesn't even mention. John always refers to himself as the "beloved," while Mark, writing Peter's account, just calls him John. Even the crucifixion accounts highlight different—although complementary—specifics. Do you find it the same with the memories you share with your girlfriends? You were both at the same party and must have seen the same people, listened to the same music, and selected food from the same table, yet she doesn't remember that the guacamole was lousy or that the playlist was heavy on Michael Jackson.

For these reasons, I queried my friends about the stories I've included. My desire was to see if the significant events in our friendship matched, to verify facts I included, and to ensure they felt my account was accurate. The conclusions I draw and opinions I offer are solely mine. What I could not have anticipated or rehearsed was the result of these interviews. Each one took a unique journey through memories and perceptions. We surprised ourselves with memories that agreed and the absence of memories for one person while the other recalled the situation so clearly. When possible, I met them in person. It was a justifiable reason to make time for connection in a too-busy schedule. The scenes of our meetings are as unique as the friendships yet while being perfectly matched to those friendships. Of course I would meet Lisa at a park and Karen C. at a restaurant, and my college roomates on-line. The scenes, natural and organic, are a true reflection of our friendships.

Each of my friends that you meet in these pages agreed to the use of their real name. This is the real deal—the good, the funny, the difficult, and the sad. While the daily interactions in each other's lives ebb and flow, my love and appreciation for each of these girlfriends is eternal.

# Chocolate-Chip Cookies

Deb made these all the time. Our deal was that she would make them if I would clean up the kitchen. Of course, we each greedily licked the dough off one beater. On occasion the dough never made it into the oven; we ate it raw.

| | |
|---|---|
| 2¼ cups flour | ¼ cup sugar |
| 1 tsp. salt | 2 eggs |
| ½ tsp. baking soda | 1 tsp. vanilla |
| 2 sticks of butter, softened | 2 cups semisweet chocolate chips |
| 1¼ cups light-brown sugar | 1 cup walnuts, chopped |

Preheat oven to 350°F. In a medium bowl, whisk flour, salt, and baking soda. Beat the butter and sugars in a separate bowl until fluffy. One at a time, beat in the eggs then the vanilla. Gradually add in the flour mixture, mixing until just combined. Mix in the chocolate chips and walnuts by hand.

Place by rounded teaspoon onto a lightly greased cookie sheet. Leave enough room for the cookies to spread. Bake eight to ten minutes. Remove when the edges are lightly browned.

Deb once added a few drops of each food coloring in our kitchen to the dough. The result was unsightly but not enough to deter us from eating them. Try it!

# Deb

*If you have a sister and she dies, do you stop saying you have one? Or are you always a sister, even when the other half of the equation is gone?*
—Jodi Picoult

The soft lighting created by cloth-covered chandeliers and crisp white table linens confused me. Round tables—normally cleared to encourage dancing—were dispersed around the rectangle of wood laminate flooring that hosted the buffet. This room, my senses screamed at me, is for celebrations. As I walked in, the confusion was overwhelming. The chatter of conversation was louder than I expected for a funeral luncheon. My husband guided me to a table where friends sat. I no longer recall which friends, but the feeling of safety permeates the years. I didn't move much from that table. I lacked the social skills to gracefully greet all the guests. At our wedding five years earlier, I had felt the same inadequacy. So I stayed put in my padded chair and offered a smile and small talk to the few guests who bravely approached to offer a kind word, squeeze my shoulder, or hug me. I know why so few approached me; what do you say to the woman who is now sisterless?

Earlier that week—Monday, in fact—I had crumbled to the cold laminate of my kitchen floor as my brother-in-law, Clayton, told me by phone that "something happened to Deb." We would learn over the next few hours that she and a coworker had been murdered at the restaurant she managed while counting inventory early that morning, her eighth wedding anniversary. As the days passed, news crews camped out in front of her house, detectives interviewed us, and we had to make funeral arrangements. In my fog and confusion, I felt clear on one subject; I needed to eulogize my sister at her funeral. It was the least I could do for a woman whom I admired and had been intimately connected to for thirty years.

In my youth I was not a chocolate lover. I preferred vanilla. My sister, however, was all about the chocolate. Eventually I tolerated treats with minimal chocolate, like vanilla cake with chocolate frosting. Then, as I approached adulthood, my appreciation for chocolate mirrored Deb's. It became commonplace for us to enjoy a chocolate treat like a thick, rich brownie when we were together. Similar to our love for chocolate, our friendship—while always grounded in sisterhood—matured over the years into a sweet harmony.

It is challenging for me to even begin to describe my sister. There is too much. Some of it seems so obvious, because she was so much of me and who I am. We were physical opposites: I was tall, and she was short, I was thin, she was curvy, my blonde hair (until I aged) contrasted her brunette locks. My most prominent physical features (height and stature) follow my dad's genetic line, while Deb resembled my mom's family. After people recovered from the shock of realizing that we were related, their next comments acknowledged how similar our laughs were and how we both gestured with our hands as we spoke. As people learned our personalities, they no longer questioned our sisterhood. We were unique and distinct while also, overlapping, and intertwined, like chocolate chips melted into a cookie.

My very first friend and my older sister by eighteen months, she was stuck with me, and I adored her. Well, except for her senior year in high school. That was a trying time for us as she spread her wings and defiantly dared anyone to try to keep her on the ground. It was hard to watch her make choices that were unhealthy and dangerous and it strained our relationship. Except for that tough year, though, I adored her.

From my mom's account, Deb was excited to meet me, her baby sister. Mom carried me into the house cradled in her arms with a stuffed black dog resting on me. She told Deb that her baby sister brought a gift for her, and Deb was sold. Good people always brought gifts. My memories and the pictures remind me that we spent all our time together. Once I was mobile we found fun wherever we went. My mom made us coordinating dresses for holidays, and we spent our Saturday mornings in pink-foam rollers in order to show off bouncy curls at church on Sunday. From this early age, Deb became my protector.

As the younger sister, at times my mere presence was annoying to Deb. Her closed bedroom door was to me, an invitation to a private meeting, not a signal that she desired privacy. The announcement that she was going to her friend's house across the street seemed like a nonverbal invitation for me to join her. It was not. Sending me on a wild-goose chase for a nonexistent item while her friends were hanging out was clearly a ruse to get me to leave.

While she aggravated me at times, I never doubted that she would defend me unflinchingly. My freshman year of high school was easier than many of my friends' since there seemed to be an invisible bubble around me at school. I did not get harassed by the upperclassmen, because I was Deb's sister. She had a reputation of being cool and tough and supremely loyal—a trait we shared.

I remember sitting in the family room one night, observing the interactions of Deb's friends: three guys and just two girls, including my sister. Varying heights and sizes, they were a mix of juniors and sophomores at our high school and, to my freshman eyes, "cool." They were not the jocks that seem to be elevated by culture no matter their moral code. These were the kids who had decided to not blend in but be strategically different. Flipped-up collars under sweaters and designer-label jeans, by day, Deb's adventurous—and slightly rebellious—spirit was awakening after school hours.

On this night the clothing was deviant: black lipstick and eyeliner for everyone, black wigs or hair colored bright red, a gold-sequined hat, and miscellaneous other items as props. The air was electrified by their excitement. Squirt guns, rice, and newspapers were packed in a bag, ready to travel. Tonight would be their initiation into the Rocky Horror Picture Show. A film made popular due to a cult following that brought the characters to life with audience participation. In awe of their courage to be seen in public dressed as they were, I stared. Granted, the movie didn't even begin playing until midnight, so most of the people who would see them were other fans. Finding reasons to be in our dinning nook and kitchen allowed me to be enveloped in their excitement for a short time. One of the older boys was cute, and I fantasized that if he just knew me a little better, the affection would be mutual. Deb, assuming the character of Magenta for the evening, was bold and devious. As they traipsed out the front door into the cool, dark evening, their electricity and my fantasy followed along like a wisp of smoke.

We would move away from these friends and into two other homes before we both settled into college, Deb at the University of Michigan and me just ten miles east at Eastern Michigan University. She began a relationship with a man who over time became controlling and jealous. Similar to other women, Deb was blind to what was obvious to those of us who cared about her. Time has wrapped the details of this experience tightly, and I struggle to remember them exactly. However, Deb must have felt attacked by both me and my mom as we constantly tried to open her eyes to the unhealthiness of her boyfriend.

Following life-altering choices, Deb's relationship with her boyfriend began to spiral out of control until they decided escaping together was their only option. She left town with him without a word to anyone. A week of unreturned phone calls finally prompted me to peek in the windows of her ground-floor apartment. There was no sign of distress but no sign of life, either. Neither my mom nor I had heard from her, so my mom asked me to file a missing person's report. I did so in a state of wonder. While answering all the questions about her—physical appearance, type of car, and last known where-a-bouts—my mind kept reeling. Am I really doing this? There were several times in my life that I was outright mad at Deb, usually because she antagonized me into a frenzy of anger. This time I was scared for her. I feared that she might never resurface in my life again.

The next I heard from her was to report that sadly, her boyfriend's behavior turned physically abusive, and Deb ended up in the hospital. She was ten hours away and didn't want help. She was tenacious and fiercely independent. A line had been crossed, and she wasn't going to allow that again. She was released to a shelter, found a new job, and secured a place to live.

Tucked away in my mementos is the card that arrived a few weeks later. Although the return address was unfamiliar, the mixed print and cursive handwriting was unmistakably Deb's. The factory greeting was humorous and alluded to being out of touch. Her personal message was task oriented at first, providing her new address and initial plans for a surprise birthday party for Mom. Then she addressed what she instinctively knew bothered me: "Listen, things are going well for me. I feel more and more like my old self every day. I know you worry, but try not to worry too much."

What a relief! Even though a restraining order was issued, the man kept harassing her for a time. But she ultimately was safe. And that new job resulted in her meeting the love of her life.

The whole family was thankful that Deb and Clayton began dating. The security of Clayton released the playful side of Deb that we hadn't seen for several years. When something fades away over time, the disappearance often goes unnoticed. Then it resurfaces like the warmth that travels through your veins from drinking hot chocolate on a cold winter day. I could sense Deb's returned playfulness on the phone and laughingly embraced it in person when Dave and I visited at Thanksgiving. Her demeanor reminded me of long-ago years before grade point averages, college entrance exams, bills, and jobs slowly allowed responsibility to seep into the space where playfulness had been present. It was the full-teeth-smile, hamming-it-up-for-photos Deb. My foodie sister who concocted a tasty snack of the oddest ingredients (melted butter, brown sugar, and cream of rice cereal) or experimented by adding a few drops of every food color to the chocolate-chip cookie dough to discover it created a camo-colored cookie. The sister who created a scavenger hunt for my thirteenth birthday party. The one who shared my love of dancing—we spent hours at it, first to the likes of Captain and Tennille and the Bee Gees on a reel-to-reel player, then graduating to blaring The Cure, INXS, and Simple Minds from our boom boxes while we danced in the living room. Deb taught me the fine art of toilet papering a friend's house and would stir me to laughter that lasted so long our bellies hurt, yet we couldn't stop. The playful Deb had returned.

Deb's life did not transform into a Disney movie with her prince whisking her away to a lavish life with peanut M&Ms in endless supply. She and Clayton both worked long, exhausting shifts at a Mexican restaurant to keep current with bills and nip away at debt. Engaging, orderly, and hardworking, Deb excelled in the restaurant business. Before she left Michigan, she had worked her way from part-time waitress to assistant manager at a college-town bistro. Arriving in Evansville, she easily found work as a waitress. While her life circumstances would keep her there for a few years, her ambition eventually propelled her to a new chain of restaurants and management.

As happens with many people, the adventure of living away from family lost its appeal. Deb again changed restaurant chains to a brand that had locations in the Detroit area. She was moving home.

It had been years since Deb and I lived in the same state, and much had changed. I had graduated college, we both were married, and Mom was surviving another rocky season with her third husband. I had always felt at a loss to help my mom in these seasons. Deb seemed to be the only person Mom would listen to. Maybe it was because she was the oldest, maybe because Mom saw herself in Deb—whatever the reason, I was relieved to have Deb back in the state to help manage the situation. She was a great buffer for my mom and me. Of course that became glaringly obvious after she died.

Deb actually had years of experience protecting us during tumultuous times. My mom tells a story of when she and Dad were arguing and it had heated up to the point where collector beer steins were being broken and dishes thrown. Deb and I were hiding behind a table in the family room when a jar with lollipops whizzed across the room. Deb waited until there seemed to be a break in the storm to scramble, grab a couple lollipops, and return to our cover. Being the younger of us had its blessings. I was sheltered from the truth by Deb and my naiveté.

One evening, after visiting Uncle Kenny (my dad's youngest brother), Deb and I were lying on the bed in our hip, deep-green Ford van that had a convertible table/bed, refrigerator, CB radio, and 8-track tape player, while my dad was at the wheel. The trip was about an hour long, and I assume we were supposed to be sleeping, since it was late. Instead of sleeping, I was lying on my back looking at the lights out the window. I was confused as to whether I was watching stars or streetlights. They looked like streetlights but kept weaving in and out of my field of view. They must be stars, I thought. I wanted to ask Deb, but she was quiet, and I sensed she didn't want to talk. Dad's driving caused us to roll back and forth across the bed and into each other which I thought was great fun. Arriving home, I went straight to bed without giving the drive another thought.

By evening the next day, my world was fatally altered by my father's death. He suffered a heart attack while clearing an area for a beach on our lakefront home. Deb and I found him, and our screams reached my mom and the whole neighborhood. Hours later my mom collected us from the neighbor's house, situated us around our oak kitchen table, and gently confirmed our suspicions. Dad had not survived.

What I would piece together years later when innocence wore off and knowing settled in was that my dad was driving drunk the night of the rolling and stargazing. He wasn't being playful, causing us to roll around, as I had assumed. He was swerving on the road and then correcting. Deb knew this then and carried it with her for years, never telling me, never shedding a negative light on my dad. It was a heavy burden for her. She, at eleven, was aware, scared, and angry, and when Dad died the next morning she lost any opportunity to confront him with her anger. In all the years between his death and her death, she did not speak angrily of my dad to me. We seemed to have an understanding that those memories are sacred and should be handled like a precious stone with white gloves, leaving no fingerprints. Due to her role as mentor and ally in my life, she did not welcome (and I did not pursue) asking her deeper questions. She took her role of protector seriously.

So much of my relationship with Deb was fueled by admiration. For a very long time, I followed her lead or direction in all the family decisions. Whom "we" were mad at. How "we" were going to make a point. In one case when we were middle-school age, Mom cooked liver (gross, I know) for dinner, and Deb informed me that "we" would not eat dinner that night. "We" were taking a stand. That may have been the first lesson I remember in the importance of knowing all the facts before you take a stand. Sensing that we would resist eating liver, Mom prepared our favorite side dishes: mashed potatoes for me and creamed corn for Deb. I was a disgruntled partner when I woke up hungry the next morning to learn that I had missed mashed potatoes.

Her laugh, I miss it terribly—loud and engaging, quiet giggling, or silent eyes dancing. And the throaty giggle, the telltale sign that she was up to something—in the back of her throat, slightly higher pitched than her fruity voice. Her tongue would lodge just inside her lower lip, which caused it to protrude. We laughed at inappropriate times and could make the other giggle with a look. Sitting across from each other at a restaurant in Boston, something set us off. I can't remember what the spark was, but we laughed uncontrollably. Our husbands smiled and questioned us. We struggled to get enough breath to answer. Slowly they succumbed to our laughter and joined in, and then they faded out while we continued on. Just like I can't remember what ignited it, I can't recall how we regained our composure. The picture of the four of us in that restaurant booth sums up a weekend of fun and laughter we enjoyed together while in Boston for our cousin's wedding.

While our times laughing were plenty, some situations required finesse and tact not normally needed between sisters. Soon after she married Clayton, Deb was delighted to be pregnant. Shortly after sharing the exciting news, Deb began to feel extreme pain in her abdomen. She made an appointment with her doctor, who discovered that the embryo was in her fallopian tube. An emergency surgery followed, resulting in her fallopian tube being removed.

While she was still recovering from the surgery, she and Clayton moved to North Carolina, where Deb started working for a new restaurant company. One afternoon she called me at work. I answered the phone in my four-foot-square cubicle, prepared to end the conversation quickly. Instead, I let out a yelp of excitement as she told me she was pregnant with twins. I was so stinkin' excited for her. The reality of having twins in the family had just begun to have weight when Deb called to share with me that she had lost the babies. The twins had reached the size of peanuts when the bleeding began. A trip to the emergency room resulted in learning that Deb was miscarrying the twins, and an emergency procedure was performed. If we lived closer, I would have been there to share her grief, cry with her, and hand her tissues. I am confident that Slurpees would have been consumed.

These losses increased my sensitivity when it came time to announce my own pregnancies. My heart ached for my sister, who continued to struggle with infertility. Since her return to Michigan, I had observed the havoc wielded on her body and psyche by the fertility drugs. While I am sure it stung, sharing the news about my first pregnancy seemed easy, probably because it was expected.

When it came time to tell Deb about my second pregnancy, I contemplated the most appropriate setting. Sharing the news in a group environment seemed unfair and callous. It would give her no opportunity to express her true feelings. Instead I suggested shopping and lunch. As we crowded around a two-person table with barely enough space to park Nate in his stroller, my anxiety revealed itself in my quietness. I began the conversation by acknowledging that hearing my news might sting and then shared that I was expecting again. She didn't delay in expressing her excitement for me and very quickly rolled into the questions about the inevitable bed rest and other consequences of a second high-risk pregnancy. Her eyes gave away only the slightest hint of…what? Frustration? Heartache? Discouragement? I would never know. She consistently only showered me and subsequently her nephews with excitement and love.

On occasion I delve into remembering Deb. She lost touch with many of her high-school and college friends over the years, but I find comfort in turning the yellowing pages of her yearbooks. A subtle smile curves my lips as faces I once knew come alive with memories of a time long past. It is a way to feel a connection to a piece of my heart that is hollow and vacant. On one such trip down nostalgia lane, amid the inscriptions and late-eighties phrases popular with teenagers, my own square-letter handwriting captured my attention.

> *Yo, Sims,*
> *Well, it's over, you're moving and I get to stay at Utica. Not a bad place better than Fla. I wish you all the best of luck at U of M. I know you'll succeed, you always do. I'm going to miss you lots. It hasn't been all roses but it hasn't been that bad!! I think it will be harder for me to adjust than you (especially w/ math). Figures you'd leave when I'm going back into Algebra. Always remember high school it will probably be the best times. I expect to be able to visit you in Ann*

*Arbor. And of course you have to visit. Especially for swim meets. I love you and depend on you much more than you know but knowing you'll be doing what you want will help me get through the "empty nest" syndrome. Keep in shape physically & mentally. You're my only "best" friend. I hope it stays that way. Live long and prosper.*

*Love always, Jo (Joanna Banana)*

If I was writing a send-off note to my sister now, nearly thirty years later, the grammar would improve while the heart of the note remained the same. The girlfriends you're about to meet and hopefully delight in as much as I do could never fill that vacancy in my heart, though I tried for five years to force it. What I ultimately learned was how unique and special each girlfriend is. Ironically it was when I met my half sister, Fran, that I released the need to fill the vacancy and celebrate the girlfriends that surrounded me. Fran entering my life awakened the reality that no one would ever replace Deb. If someone with shared blood and genetics didn't, no one would. What a blessed relief.

# Chocolate Dream Bars

When I found this recipe in Deb's collection, I instantly remembered the sweetness of a similar Christmas treat that Lisa and I enjoyed from a friend's mom. Memories from a time filled with dreams washed over me.

| Crust | Topping | |
|---|---|---|
| 1 cup flour | 1 cup brown sugar | 12 oz. chocolate chips |
| ½ cup brown sugar | 2 tbsp. flour | 1 tsp. vanilla |
| ½ cup butter | ½ tsp. baking powder | 2 eggs, slightly beaten |
| | ¼ tsp. salt | |

Preheat oven to 300°F. Mix flour and sugar. With a pastry blender, cut butter into flour mixture until pieces are the size of peas. Pat into an eight-by-sixteen inch cookie sheet. Bake for twenty minutes.

While baking, prepare topping. Mix first five ingredients. Add vanilla to eggs and blend into brown sugar mixture. Carefully spread the mixture over the slightly browned crust. Return to oven and bake at 300° for fifteen to twenty minutes. Cool and then cut into small squares.

# LISA

*Friends are the siblings God never gave us.*
*—Mencius*

The water was like glass, with the sun's rays piercing through and reflecting the warmth and light. Lisa's dog yanked on the leash as soon as she spotted the water.

"Where do you want to sit?" Lisa asked me.

We chose a spot close to the path, since we were the only visitors enjoying the solitude on this gorgeous fall day.

We both had bags with our supplies. They were perfect reflections of our personalities. Mine was filled with a wet suit, two towels, other miscellaneous swim paraphernalia, and the salad I had brought for lunch. Simple and minimalist. Lisa, prepared for comfort and any need that might arise, unzipped her backpack and retrieved her plastic-coated blanket and a toy for her Goldendoodle, Flower. As we spread her blanket in the shade of a tree at a safe distance from the water, avoiding Flower's splashing, I prepared for a conversation that would require us to visit tough memories as well as relive ones that still brought the sweet sound of laughter.

A few weeks earlier, I had explained to Lisa the purpose of this book and asked her to dredge up memories of our friendship. While she agreed, I could see doubt and hesitation crease her brow. She feared this exercise might turn out to be fruitless. Whether we accomplished my goal or not, it would still be time well spent with the friend who has known me the longest.

Although we didn't meet until chemistry class in our junior year of high school, Lisa and I shared similar lives. We both lacked a steady father figure, moved often, and had very liberal "rules" in our homes. Considering the turbulence and angst of high school, it was a gift that we connected and have remained allies in this life. Very quickly our friendship grew, and she was enveloped into my group of friends and family. In high school we can't imagine life without these friends; however, as we grow and experience new challenges and opportunities, some friendships fade away. Ours stayed intact. We survived parental desertion, medical issues, deaths, marriages, and child-rearing. Through it all Lisa had my back.

She seemed the obvious choice to fill the hole Deb left. After all, besides my family she knew me the longest. She was virtually a member of our family. My sister loved her and teased Lisa just as much as she teased did me. When Lisa's mom left in the winter of our senior year, my stepfather offered to adopt her so that she would be eligible for the benefits his dependents received, which included college tuition. And besides Deb, she was the friend who knew all my yuckiest secrets and still loved me. We were nearly inseparable through high school. If we had free time, we were together.

Naturally we agreed to an annual camping trip that our group of friends took each summer. The site was remote, so we had to hike all our gear about a half mile down a trail to the campsite on the river's edge. It was a site that one of our friend's older brothers had been using since they were in high school. The brothers had graduated not only from high school but also from rustic camping. Since we were in high school, inexperienced, and know-it-alls, we naturally brought too much gear, and mostly the wrong gear. Knowing we would have to hike all our gear in, the consensus was to share one tent for our group of seven, thereby reducing our load. Three boys and four girls would occupy the aging canvas tent borrowed from a dad. It came complete with a musty odor and a door that didn't fully close. Our other essentials were a tape player, the requisite mix tapes, batteries for the tape player, bathing suits, Oreos, and Pop-Tarts. Oh, Lisa brought toilet paper. She was always prepared.

With the blithe attitude that high schoolers embrace so fervently, we camped. We laughed. We swung off the rope swing into the river. Lisa chickened out, didn't release the rope, swung back to the bluff, and upon landing caught her big toe nail on a root, ripping it right off. Someone did remember the Band-Aids, thank God. The music played until "o'dark thirty," and sporadically each of us made our way to our sleeping bag. Several hours before sunrise I awoke, and a sigh of contentment escaped me as I remembered my environment. Then shock and disgust overwhelmed me as the smell trapped in the tent alarmed my senses. Oh, those boys were stinky.

Over the years, on that river's bluff, we laughed and cried with each other, raged against injustice and our parents, and created memories that easily resurface even twenty-five years later.

The summer after we graduated high school, we both landed jobs at a local water park. Each of our parents had left town. Not just for a weekend or the summer; they were far away permanently. I was living at a mutual friend's house until it was time to move into my dorm, and Lisa was staying with her mom's ex-boyfriend. (What???? While I have the fondest memories of this summer, my parent brain is exploding!) I was eighteen and making all my own decisions, many of them poor. Thank goodness social media couldn't permanently record our antics. Our time at the water park seemed too fun to get paid for. Lisa was a ride operator, and I was at the admission gate. We diligently attempted to coordinate our lunch breaks when we worked the same shift. On slow days I readily offered to fill in for an absent employee if it meant I could be at the same ride as Lisa.

One late afternoon a storm rolled in while Lisa and I were working a water ride. The ride closed for safety reasons, and we crowded into the small life-jacket hut with several other coworkers, taking refuge from the storm and laughing the time away. The friends we made that summer at the water park were due to Lisa's welcoming personality. Quiet and reserved, I would have drawn a much smaller and more shallow circle of friends on my own. I benefited from the way Lisa enveloped others into our activities while never casting me aside.

Through the years we have shared agonies and disappointments, and at times we have hidden parts of our lives from each other. But through it all we shared something greater: hope. Neither of us dwelled in a victim mentality, bemoaning the instability of our families. I have always felt fortunate that God would pair me with a person who could understand my situation but not judge or dwell in it.

Whenever there was a crisis, we rallied around each other, solved the issue, supported each other, and then moved on.

We each had a turn putting our friendship to the fire with men. Interestingly enough, both situations involved deception and coming clean. Lisa's clandestine relationship was uncovered by a mutual friend who then coordinated the reveal to me. I was hurt and shocked and ended up leaving our hangout for a short time to process my feelings. My overriding emotion was feeling left out. I was the last of our tight-knit group of friends to know of the relationship. That didn't feel good. When I returned to the room, Lisa answered my questions, and life moved on. We had just graduated high school, and like any girls worth their weight, drama spiked and sank regularly. Ironically, painted on the wall above our heads was our guiding phrase, "Be excellent to each other."

My relationship reveal seemed much more difficult, perhaps because I was the one unraveling a web of lies. One evening Lisa and I met at Ruby Tuesday to enjoy our favorite salad bar. As we waited at the bar for a table to become available, I broached the subject. The timing was critical, since in six weeks we would depart for a trip we had planned over the last few months. The words I put together escape me, but I have never been known for eloquence, so I am confident my confession was blurted out to Lisa. I do remember the hurt look on her face. Not long before this conversation she had shared her hope that she and Dave—yes, the person I was now committed to and would eventually marry—would restore their relationship. In our talk by the lake twenty-one years later, Lisa told me that she'd had an idea that Dave loved me a month or so before that conversation at the bar, but it was hard to accept. While my impression was that Lisa was hurt because of the relationship, it turns out her wounds were caused by the same emotion that had struck me five years earlier. She felt left out. In both situations our normal rhythm of talking every day about absolutely everything was disrupted. That disruption, however temporary, was unsettling.

That night she bravely endured dinner, which had a marked decrease in conversation, and then decided to go home for the evening instead of continuing with our plans. Understandable. Time heals wounds and tempers disappointments. Thankfully Lisa agreed to continue with our Colorado adventure since it was already paid for. In hindsight the trip, while awkward at first, forced us to move past that hurdle and back into our normal rhythm.

Living life together was our normal rhythm. Moving beyond those difficult experiences, forgiving each other, and being happy for the other solidified our friendship. We were honor attendants in each other's weddings. She cleaned my house for me while I was on bed rest. I listened as she secretly shared how she had fallen in love with one of our high-school friends. She organized food and took care of my family as we publicly grieved at Deb's funeral. I encouraged her through the first night she held her baby and he was fussy. When I was away for Nathan's sixth birthday, she decorated his room and made sure he felt celebrated. We laughed, we cried, we called each other's bluff. That was our normal rhythm.

Our phone calls aren't daily anymore; they are sporadic at best. We carve out time twice a year for a meal. We live too far apart to pop over to borrow sugar or a table and chairs. Our time is spent on our husbands and kids and, in Lisa's case, constant home improvement. However busy and distant our lives seem, our hearts are forever connected. When we see each other, nothing has changed, even though everything has. Like sisters who unquestionably take the good times with the disappointments, Lisa and I have weathered many storms.

Friendships formed in the narcissistic stage of life are tenuous at best and a wonderful surprise when they survive and thrive. Never underestimate the value of a friend who has been through your best and worst moments. There comes a time when you realize that a friendship will continue for a lifetime, not just a season. For this, I am thankful.

# No-Bake Cookies

Deb and I made no-bake cookies regularly on summer days. In college, my roommates and I were probably too busy to make cookies, but these simple cookies would have been a favorite for one reason: peanut butter!

| 3 cups oatmeal | 3 tbsp. cocoa powder | ½ cup butter |
| --- | --- | --- |
| 1½ cups sugar | ½ cup milk | ½ cup peanut butter |

Bring sugar, cocoa, butter, and milk to a boil in large pot. Boil for two minutes. Stir in peanut butter and oatmeal. Remove from heat and spoon onto wax paper in small piles. Let cool. EAT!

## Sue, Sheri, & Nanette

*We didn't realize we were making memories. We just knew we were having fun.*
*—Unknown*

"Oh Lord, help me. I don't like the nineteen-year-old me very much," began Sue's e-mail.

Our calendars are too full now and our group has spread out geographically, so we are unable to talk in person. I would have loved to sit down, the four of us again, to dredge up memories and rehash perceptions. Instead I have a picture pinned to my board near my writing space. What I am drawn to is our smiles; in this photo they are big, brilliant, and genuine. The photo was taken many years post college when all of us were married; our husbands and kids in another room. It was a time when we thought life would never be different or better.

One email to Sue, Sheri and Nanette, to stimulate their memories and glean their perspective on our friendship, initiated a buzz of replies. I read the first responses on my phone while sitting in the pickup lane at my sons' high school. I laughed and cried and laughed again, unconcerned at the looks from other waiting parents. Flashbacks of good times, raw honesty, and crazy choices flooded my soul, and I was reminded how I miss these women immensely. We lived through so much together. I am sad that our lives are lived so separately now. We all have changed significantly since our college years, yet we kept the core personalities that drew us together. We traveled some difficult roads together and made choices that stung, but through it all we protected something special.

As new suitemates our melding wasn't seamless. Sheri and Nanette came as a package innocently delivered for my sophomore year of college. I had arrived to our dorm room first, since I was an orientation leader for the incoming freshmen, and chose the bedroom for me and my roommate, Heather, by hastily piling boxes and suitcases into the corner. I spent the next few days engulfed in training and spending time with my boyfriend, which meant minimal time in my room, resulting in nothing unpacked on freshman move-in day.

st day of orientation, I brought the group of doe-eyed freshman to my suite to show them an upperclassman dorm floor plan. As I opened the door, I thought I was in the wrong room. The furniture was arranged, pictures were hung, and there was a personal touch to one side of our common space. A quick look in the other bedroom revealed full yet neat closets, freshly made beds, and desks adorned with various supplies. My new suitemates had arrived.

Over the next several weeks, I learned that my new suitemates were high-school best friends, had boyfriends, and were very studious. They learned that across the hall were Sue and Mara, my suitemates from last year, and that we would have preferred to room together.

Someone hatched the plan for the smokers of our freshman foursome to always light up in my suite to annoy these new freshmen and get them to request a room change. None of us remember who devised the plan, but it was on. Not only would the smokers camp out in my room, but if Sheri and Nanette were gone, they would blow smoke into their closet. Shameful! As if the smoking wasn't bad enough, Sue's roommate, Mara, walked across the hall to my suite in order to call home, which meant hours-long calls that tied up the phone line. Nanette shares now that she was ready to move out, but Sheri wouldn't hear of it. Instead Sheri retaliated by endearing herself to us. We weren't completely ruthless. From the start we included Sheri and Nanette in our plans. Sheri was more likely to join us, and eventually our foursome from the prior year became a happy family of six for a while.

It seems food and health have always been tightly woven in our friendship. Surprisingly I was not the healthy one. Nanette was the driving force in making healthy choices. I think she may have even had a blender to mix protein shakes in our dorm room. Most of this was escalated by her position on the cheerleading team. They had to weigh in every week, and a pound difference was detrimental. Attempting to be healthy, Sue, Sheri, and I obsessed on a *fromage* sandwich. Thick slices of crusty white bread layered with sprouts, lettuce, tomato, and the namesake cheese became the reason for regular stops at the campus deli.

While Nanette was very disciplined, my roommate began sneaking food from all of us. She had completed a liquid diet—yes, the one of Oprah fame—over the summer and was reintroducing solid food that fall. After several months of finding empty boxes of crackers and cookies in our storage area, we set some traps and realized that she was binge eating our food. We were inconvenienced, for sure, but our true concern was for her health. It was decided that I should lead the intervention while Sheri and Nanette listened through their closet wall. In the right timing they would join the conversation to affirm our concern for her health. While the circumstance was serious and unpleasant, it served as a cementing situation for our friendship. We learned that we could depend on each other and work together.

My athletic endeavors had taken a backseat since quitting the swim team my freshman year. While I would swim occasionally on my own, I regretted my decision to quit and actively avoided seeing the coach or other swimmers. Since swimming was the only way I knew to work out, it was easier to do nothing. By the winter of our sophomore year, Sue, Sheri, and I—probably inspired by Nanette—began walking the track at the university recreation building. Our reasons were as varied as the people we saw there. I needed it to combat the dark, brooding thoughts I harbored about myself in the aftermath of a devastating breakup. This carried over to the following fall when we assembled a coed flag football team led by Nanette and her new boyfriend, a high-school friend of Sue's, who she eventually married.

While Nanette encouraged us to be healthier by her example, Sue was the cool one, calm in every circumstance and consistently armed with a cheeky remark. One morning of her freshman year, a male swimmer walked into class proudly wearing his new letter jacket. With her trademark sarcasm, Sue quipped loud enough for him to hear, "Nice jacket." Years later, when Dave and I became friends, we all laughed as he called her out for that remark. It was him those years ago in the letter jacket and her sarcasm had seared into his memory.

"I remember there was a lot of talk about Sue," Sheri wrote in her response to my e-mail. "Everyone on the floor loved Sue, and everyone knew her. My expectations were very high when I met her because she was so beloved. Most of the times when my expectations are that high, I am disappointed. But I wasn't. Sue lived up to the hype."

This is high praise from Sheri. The skeptic of our group, Sheri had nothing to prove and no one to impress. Her high-school boyfriend attended the same college, so she was secure while the rest of us were still figuring out how to be ourselves. While my role as confronter—authenticated by my intervention with the snack stealer—continued, I had also been dubbed the bad influence by some parents. It was a convenient role for my roommates to let me assume. If anything went wrong, or if parents saw something in our apartment that shocked them, like a balcony half-filled with beer cans needing to be recycled, it was easy to blame me. Like I drank all that beer on my own. Sheesh!

While the fun and hilarious memories are plentiful and it is always amusing to relive them in our conversations, this friendship, like any with longevity, had to survive tough circumstances. As decisions concerning living arrangements for the following year needed to happen, we were in a quandary. Sheri and Nannette were obviously sticking together, my roommate had decided to live on her own, and Sue was still partnered with her roommate from the previous two years. Finding an affordable, clean apartment for five people was difficult. Sue's roommate, Mara, mentioned that she had a friend from home who could be our sixth. That would work out great since we had toured a two-story two-bedroom apartment that could easily hold six of us, as long as we (meaning our dads) built bunk beds. To us college students, this apartment seemed luxurious. A galley kitchen, dining area, large living room with a balcony, and even a nook for a bar comprised the main floor, while up the spiral staircase were the two bedrooms and a bathroom. The cost was minimal, since we split everything, including the utilities, among six people. As with most situations, we enjoyed the honeymoon phase of this arrangement for several months, and then the realities of six women—some with boyfriends—eroded the situation.

The main cause of discontent was the two boyfriends who would sleep on our living room floor until afternoon. While we roommates got up for classes or jobs, several days a week the guys were lumps on the floor that began to look a lot like freeloaders. Discontentment rose to such a level that I began opening the shades and turning on the television when I returned from my morning class as if the guys weren't even there. My behavior was bold and boorish, out of character for me.

One evening Sheri and Nanette pulled me into the bedroom we shared and urged me to confront Mara and her friend about this freeloading. I suppose I hesitated because I do not like confrontation; however, I also bristle against injustice. Sheri and Nanette were convincing, so I called the two women upstairs while Sheri and Nanette remained in our bedroom, listening at the door.

Standing in the small landing at the top of the stairs with the bedroom doors in front of me, the bathroom to the right, and a wall at my back, I began what I hoped would be a civil conversation. Our requests were simply that Mara and her friend pay a larger share of the utilities and rent to cover for their boyfriends and that the boyfriends not camp out in our living space all day. Mara's friend, instantly inflamed, aggressively cornered me with my back to the cast-iron banister of the stairs. I remember staying calm outwardly and inwardly hoping that Sheri and Nanette would save me before she pushed me over to tumble down the stairs. They told me later that they were tracking the situation through the cracked open bedroom door. They assured me they would have protected me from falling if needed.

This situation of course changed the atmosphere in our apartment. The entertaining times of the fall—extra-large pizzas and dance parties after flag football games—gave way to a quieter living space and forced politeness.

What happens when the person tagged in your group as the bearer of bad news becomes the subject of it? A new town crier must be identified, and the unfortunate role is forced upon another. Our network of friends was wide. Each of us had friends outside our tight web, and those friends knew each other at varying levels of association, so word of my boyfriend's infidelity was passed along until it landed at Sheri's doorstep. She was months away from marrying her man and knee deep in wedding details. I am sure this was the last situation she wanted on her plate.

"I remember feeling very strongly about telling you," she told me in our email conversation. "No one wanted to, but I thought you should know, so I just did it." My boyfriend's behavior affronted her strong sense of justice.

Her exact words elude me, but the scene is seared in my memory. Sitting in our room, side by side on the lower bunk, she told me how one friend witnessed my bozo boyfriend's antics with another coed. Then another person confirmed the cheating. I stiffened with the shock of the news but wasn't altogether surprised.

Sheri remembers me responding, "Yeah, I know; no big deal." We both knew I was more hurt than I let on. He wasn't the first boyfriend to cheat on me. I was jaded. I left abruptly to process my response and decide my next move. I was never angry with Sheri for telling me. My respect for her courage is a cornerstone in our friendship.

The four of us weaved in and out of each other's lives in the years post college. Sheri married her high school sweetheart and had kids first; she was our poster child for settling down and managing a family. Her husband's job dictated their move out of Michigan. Within a few years' time, the rest of us married. Nanette and I eventually lived just a mile apart, while Sue moved just over the border of Michigan to Toledo.

As the miles grew, we made concerted efforts to visit. One May, Sue, Nanette, and I planned a surprise trip to Sheri's to celebrate her thirtieth birthday. Her husband made sure she would be home as we pulled into her driveway on a Friday. We went shopping, had a nice dinner, exchanged beauty tips, and shared a million or more words. Our visit was so enjoyable we spoke of repeating it annually. We didn't anticipate that the trip a few years later to an Indiana spa would be our last.

When I say spa, dial back your expectations about 50 percent. While the spa itself was pleasant, the building was near the freeway, and the advertised nature trails and tranquil lake were overstated. No matter; we were together, and, more significantly for me, this retreat fell on the one-year anniversary of Deb's death. I had no idea what to expect on this day, so being away from all things familiar, save my friends, seemed agreeable.

Since Nanette was the person who ignited the runner in me, it was fitting that we chose to run together on Saturday morning. While the other two moaned at us for moving around the hotel room early, we laced up our shoes and left the room. Since the nature trails were short and not well marked, our route took many turns as we attempted to find roads safe for running. Near the end of our run, sorrow and anguish overwhelmed me, and I stooped over, wracked with dry tears, unable to catch my breath. Somehow I moved again, and to this day I am washed with a sense of sorrow that Nanette had to experience my pain, though I am also grateful that she was there with me in my anguish.

Later that evening, while sitting on the balcony, there was a foreign tenseness among us. We moved around in the white plastic chairs, their stiff feel reflecting our mood. We just couldn't get comfortable in the chairs or with each other. While the intention was to meet up every year or two, it never happened again. The simplest of explanations is the busyness of life, but in reality our friendship was changing, and in the new season it was not the priority it once was.

The four of us lived so much life together. We shared some of the toughest moments in our young adult lives: Nanette's divorce, Deb's murder, Sue's dad's cancer diagnosis and death. I felt an intimacy with them so strong that I purposefully avoided making eye contact with them as I eulogized my sister. Seeing them hurt for me would have crumpled me. While we easily slip back into conversations with each other, they are stretched years apart. I suppose we could each name reasons for the slow fade of communication. For me, while I love them dearly, they aren't part of my everyday routine, and I don't rely on them as I used to, which of course is the reason that this lovely trio could not fill the hole in my heart created by my sister's death. However, they are the type of girlfriends everyone needs: those who support you as you fall apart and then pull you up and make you engage life again.

# Forgotten Kisses

I love finding my sister's handwritten notes on recipes, a habit instilled by our grandmother. "Turned out good. Very easy," tops the page of this recipe. It mirrors how I feel about Karen.

| | |
|---|---|
| 3 egg whites | ¾ tsp. vanilla |
| ¾ tsp. cream of tartar | 2 cups semisweet chocolate chips |
| ¼ tsp. salt | 3 drops red food coloring (optional) |
| 1–1½ cups sugar | |

Preheat oven to 375°F. Spray cookie sheets with nonstick spray. Beat egg whites until frothy. Add cream of tartar and salt. Beat until very stiff. Add sugar slowly by teaspoonful. Beat until glossy. Fold in vanilla, chips, and food coloring (if using). Drop by spoonful onto greased sheet. Place in oven. Turn off the oven and leave overnight or until oven is cold. The meringues will turn gummy if you open the oven door to peek.

# Karen

*Distance means so little when someone means so much.*
*—Unknown*

A flight to Denver to spend one day with my girlfriend from California was a dream that we couldn't work out. Instead we squeezed in an hour-long phone call between an orthodontist appointment, a book club meeting, and preparing dinners.

"I am sorry to be short, but I only have an hour," I began our conversation.

We took a few minutes to brief each other. She had interviewed for a job but turned it down. The role wasn't a fit. I filled her in on the extremely busy yet exciting season I was living. As our conversation progressed, we often offered a contrasting opinion to what the other said. As I reflected on our conversation, it occurred to me that we see each other truer than we see ourselves. We certainly give each other more grace.

Several summers ago I gave a piece of my heart away. It's not the first time. I am a pretty tenderhearted person, and pieces of my heart are often pulled; many times they break off. Sometimes it's a seemingly insignificant commercial. Many times it has to do with children who are living in horrible conditions or have been scarred by decisions made by people who are supposed to protect them. Most times it has to do with my own childrens' choices that sting and I can't save them from. This time it was because I had to say good-bye to a dear friend.

My friendship with Karen developed almost instantly, even though our first meeting was at a stressful time in both our lives. Karen remembers an e-mail conversation beginning due to a misdirected e-mail she sent to me. I don't recall if I realized it was sent in error, but my response was super nice, according to Karen, and we continued to e-mail about our upcoming weddings.

The day before her wedding and three weeks prior to mine was our first in-person interaction. I was a bit hesitant at the meeting. I hoped we would get along. After all, our husbands were good friends; wouldn't they choose wives who were similar in their hobbies and tendencies? As we all know, that is not always the case. Karen was rushing off on a prewedding errand while a group of us were leaving for a local rock-climbing area. Yes, rock-climbing the day before the wedding. The morning of our wedding, Dave went mountain biking. It's just the kind of couples we are. It's no surprise that our kids' first experience whitewater rafting was together. Crazy attracts crazy. Anyway, that first meeting was a brief introduction on the sidewalk in front of Karen's townhouse, and then we were both off. While I understood Karen's brevity due to getting married the next day, she felt she left me with the impression that she was self-centered.

The location of the wedding ceremony and reception reflected California culture. The church was Mediterranean architecture and the reception held in a garden setting. An outdoor wedding in May in Michigan is risky, but in California they had beautiful weather. We apparently had similar tastes, because every detail I observed made me think, this could be my wedding. Of course I saw her and chatted with her for a bit at their reception. Karen was a very hospitable bride and made sure to spend time with all her guests.

Because their reception was early in the day and their honeymoon flight didn't depart until the next morning, a small crowd of friends invaded their suite at the hotel by the airport. I was told we were invited, but Karen assured me that it was a "fantastic surprise" to her when we all arrived. Upon their arrival at the hotel in their fancy wedding clothes, the hotel upgraded Karen and Dave to the presidential suite. The upgraded suite included a baby grand piano, two kitchens, and plenty of room for our group. We spent the next several hours sharing laughs and sing-a-longs while the best man, Joe, played the piano. It was an unexpected blessing when Karen and I were able to sit and chat in a quiet corner of the suite.

The next time we saw each other was at my wedding. Even though I'd only known Karen a short amount of time, I remember the feeling of disappointment when I discovered that I would not be able to hang out with her and her husband when they came into town the week before my big day since I already had planned one last girls weekend. Beyond pulling her husband onto the dance floor, I did not spend any quality time with them during our reception since I am not a skilled hostess, especially at big events like a wedding.

My work took me out west several times over the next year, and Karen and I always managed to meet up and spend some time together. One hilarious night someone's sense of direction was a bit mixed up, and we agreed to walk to a coffee house that was "one or two blocks away." After seven or eight blocks, we ended up jumping in a cab to discover the coffee house was several miles away.

During this time period, we began planning a trip together. We finally agreed upon a cycling tour of Banff National Park. We were excited and about to reserve our spots when two of the most opposing life circumstances occurred: Karen's father-in-law passed away, and I found out that I was pregnant. A great example of how God works in our lives even before we commit our lives to Him. His providence saved us from being in another country when Karen needed to support her husband's family and saved me from a potential miscarriage.

Thirteen years, four kids, two moves, and a lot of life later, we finally vacationed together. Our families traveled from opposite sides of the country and met at Yellowstone National Park. For three laugh-filled, adventure-seeking, busy days, we forgot the distance that normally separates us. Our kids—four boys—mesh like they are cousins. Our husbands are high-school friends, like minded and share a deep interest in all things cycling. The day we were to meet up, they were driving in from Jackson Hole, and we were arriving from Rapid City, South Dakota, so we knew the chances of arriving at the same time were very slim. Assuming they would arrive first, I had put our lodge reservations in Karen's name. As we made the long trek through the mountains, my eagerness became harder to control. Being in the mountains, we did not have reliable cell signals, so we had difficulty even checking in with each other. At one point we did have a brief conversation, and Karen told me that they had some issues that needed to be addressed, so they would be arriving later than expected.

We arrived, parked, and made our way to the check-in building. Whom do we see waiting outside? Karen's husband, also named Dave, so I call him Wisser. I gave him a quick hug, said hi to their boys, and asked where Karen was. Wisser told me, "She's inside checking in."

I was through the door in a flash, and in four quick steps—really Tigger-like bounces—I was at her side. The desk clerk was patient as we hugged, laughed, and talked over each other. We were so excited to be together again.

Yellowstone National Park is an amazing place. We saw a variety of wildlife and many natural wonders. We viewed amazing sunsets and thunderstorms that are unique to that altitude. Karen and I strategized how to protect our boys from grizzlies and we were amazed by the plate sized pancakes served at the park restaurant. The visit's sweetness was more robust due to sharing it with my friend.

On our last day together, we hiked to a secluded rock big enough for our families to sit on and admire the beauty of the lake at the base of the Tetons. The boys quickly began exploring the shoreline and discovered that the lake, fed by spring water and melted snow, was very cold. Karen and I laughed at our husbands, watched wildlife, and dragged everything out as long as possible to avoid our last stop and the good-bye that was inevitable. We did a pretty good job. We didn't stop for the "last supper" until six that evening. We lingered at Taco Bell, a tradition for the husbands, and then at the gas station next door much longer than necessary. Beyond pumping gas, using the restroom, and purchasing snacks, there isn't much else to do except delay the inevitable.

My eyes had been filled with tears since dinner, and now they overflowed. The heartache settled in. My heart was already losing a piece that would fall out when we eventually separated. The conversation seemed to be a little more forced at first as we tried to mask our emotions. Then I think our husbands had a foreboding of the tears to come and began telling funny stories from their years of knowing and traveling together. But the time did eventually come for hugs and high-fives and "safe travels" and good-byes. As we drove away, my tears flowed for close to an hour—soft, steady tears that I tried to stop but just couldn't. Karen shared that as they drove away she wondered, "Are we wasting a lifetime by living apart?"

Constantly through the years, we have questioned why we don't live near each other.

Our family still had five days of travel and exploration ahead of us, and we had a blast. As much as we tried, we were not able to convince Karen's family to join us. Similarly, they invited us to follow them west instead of heading east, but we each had obligations that kept us on our predetermined path.

As the weeks after that vacation turned to months, the hole in my heart was repaired. Like always, life fills in the gaps. Then another friend sent me a book she really wanted me to read. In this book the author eloquently described her profound hurt and loss when a close friend moved across the country from her. The wound was reopened as the feelings from the gas station in Idaho Falls surfaced. I cried more tears and longed to have my friend by my side again. I called her a few days later and told her of the renewed sense of longing, and we both agreed that we didn't know why we weren't neighbors. Why couldn't we find a way to live closer? Upon further reflection I realized what a gift God had given us in each other. Because of the distance, infrequent visits, and busyness of life, we cherished our friendship so much more. But it's not the same as seeing her expression as she tells a story about a happening in her life.

"There is safety in a friend who is not in your everyday realm," Karen mentioned.

Karen is symmetrical to me. Not physically—I am tall and she is not, and she has lovely golden-blond hair that stays where it's put, as opposed to my part-curly-part-straight, brown-quickly-going-gray mess. However, similar circumstances hurt our hearts. For instance, we are gentle and quiet until you wrong our boys. Then the momma bear instincts roar. We laugh easily and tear up just as quickly. Slow processors, we need time to weigh out all the implications before giving thoughtful answers or make a decision. Being outside and enjoying nature soothes our souls. We'd rather follow but will lead if no one else steps up or if everything is falling apart. While Karen would easily have filled many places in my heart left empty from the loss of my sister, she was just too far away.

I was a wimp about telling Karen that Deb had died. Dave and I had planned a family vacation to California in early September 2002. Airline tickets were purchased and the itinerary set months before Deb died. On the docket was spending a few days with Karen and Dave, visiting my aunt and uncle, and hopefully seeing other friends and relatives as we introduced our boys—ages two and three—to California. Since Karen and Dave weren't local, I felt there was no need to tell them immediately about my sister. Yes, that was a lousy reason to exclude them. In my fog of grief, the weeks passed, and a few weeks before our trip, I realized abruptly that I needed to tell Karen. It was incredibly awkward for me, since I felt like a loser for not telling her earlier. Also, Deb's death was still so raw that I had a difficult time verbalizing any thoughts about it.

Graciously, Karen was not hurt, but she was surprised that I could hold all the emotion in. Our conversation on the phone was short. Both of us were too young and inexperienced in these types of situations to know what to say. In California, however, we found ourselves sitting on the fifty-yard line of a local football field, my boys running around erratically and her infant, Ryan, blissfully unaware as my symmetrical friend listened while I relayed the details of my hurt and abject emptiness. When our husbands returned from their mountain bike ride we enjoyed an excellent meal at a crowded, noisy, authentic Mexican restaurant.

Karen and her family visited us in Michigan one summer. When they parked their rental car in front of our home, my boys busted out our front door, yelling, "The Wissers are here! The Wissers are here." I feel that enthusiasm each time we talk, and when the call ends, a contented sigh escapes between my lips. What I realized recently, when I learned after the fact that Karen's sister-in-law and father had died within weeks of each other, was that our closeness is not directly related to an everyday intimacy. We have a common admiration for each other in how we choose to live our lives. Our symmetry leads me to believe Karen could fill my need for a sister. While special and unique, however, it is not a replacement.

# Rocky-Road Bars

My sister added a purple sticky tab to the page containing this recipe in *The Great American Cookie Book,* which I inherited after she died. That tab meant she intended to make the cookies. I snicker at the appropriateness of the title linking me and Debra Sue. Rocky aptly describes our relationship and bars are a staple dessert for Debra Sue's family in Iowa.

| 2 cups semisweet chocolate chips | 1 cup sugar | 2 eggs |
|---|---|---|
| 1½ cups flour | 6 tbsp. butter, soft | 2 cups minimarshmallows |
| 1½ tsp. baking powder | 1½ tsp. vanilla | 1½ cups walnuts, chopped |

Preheat oven to 375°F. Melt one cup of chocolate chips until smooth. Cool to room temperature. In a small bowl, combine flour and baking powder. Beat sugar, butter, and vanilla in a large bowl until crumbly. Beat in eggs. Add melted chocolate and beat until smooth. Gradually beat in flour mixture. Spread batter into greased thirteen-by-nine-inch pan. Bake for sixteen to twenty minutes until wooden pick inserted in center comes out slightly sticky. Remove from oven and immediately sprinkle with marshmallows, nuts, and remaining chocolate chips. Return to oven for two minutes. Remove from oven; cool in pan on wire rack.

## Debra Sue

*Yesterday is not ours to recover, but tomorrow is ours to win or lose.*
—*Lyndon B. Johnson*

She turned into the galley kitchen from the dining room as I entered from the other end. With the smallest movement of her eyes, she shared with me a look that signaled, "Now?" With the most minute change of my facial expression, I acknowledged yes. Turning on her heel, she headed out in the same direction she had entered, while I turned back to the direction I had entered to quickly grab my notebook.

We met in the living room. We had been here a few hours earlier with the same purpose in mind: the interview. Then, we leisurely settled across from each other into the soft sage sofas on the subtly decorated area rug. Debra Sue was backlit by the late-afternoon light cascading in the window. The room, shadowed by that fading light, distracted me as I tried to remember where the light switch was located. Saving me from my distraction, Debra Sue pulled the chain on a mission-style table lamp and illuminated the sitting area.

Beginning with a catch-up session, Debra Sue had shared a current trial she was experiencing. But within ten minutes we were joined by other family members (it was Thanksgiving Day, after all). The conversation bounced over many topics, as is normal with family, especially women. I sensed that it wasn't the appropriate time to delve into the interview. Before long it was time to put the finishing touches on our holiday meal. As we moved to do so, my concern that it would be nearly impossible to find alone time to conduct this interview on Thanksgiving was becoming reality.

So now, after dinner, just before Debra Sue assumed the same position on the same sofa, I suggested we move to her husband's office. A knowing smile and agreement happened quickly, and we settled into black office chairs surrounded by pictures of John's fishing charters.

I had been apprehensive preparing for this interview. Frustratingly, this is one relationship that was a rocky road. Living 160 miles apart had certainly created a natural distance in our relationship, but there was more. An invisible tension has invaded us over the years and created a heightened level of what Debra Sue aptly described as cautiousness between us.

Our first meeting was a rainy Mother's Day weekend on a small island in Lake Erie. Kelley's Island is a vacation destination, and only a few hundred people are permanent residents. Dave and I arrived by ferry—the only way to reach the island—and waited at the marina for Debra Sue and her husband John, who owned a boat. When each new boat approached the busy marina, I anxiously asked Dave if it was theirs. Eventually Dave spotted them and waved as they pulled alongside the dock. There was only time for a quick greeting as we piled into their eighteen-foot Critchfield to go for a ride.

Older than Dave by three years and his only sibling, Debra Sue was a woman I wanted to impress. I subconsciously believed that if she liked me, I would fare better with Dave's parents. Dave had talked about me to his sister while they were skiing a few months prior. During our interview, Debra Sue told me she remembered being anxious to meet me following that conversation.

John gave us a tour around the island by boat, and then we docked and drove to the trailer Debra Sue had rented for the weekend. While Dave and I had no expectations about our housing, she was aware that the trailer, while clean, was, well, a trailer. My down-to-earth reaction to go with the flow helped ease any anxiety for both of us. The fact that we were both comfortable in our rental boded well for us.

After we settled in, we drove into the small town to enjoy dinner and drinks at a restaurant overlooking the water. The conversation was lively and pleasant. The band playing cover songs was loud. Debra Sue and John were (and are) superb hosts, never lacking for conversation.

A defining moment for me happened while standing in line for the women's restroom. As usual for women, Debra Sue and I ventured together to the facilities, and as the door opened, I glimpsed that the bathroom was equipped with two toilets, but neither was surrounded by stall walls or doors. We essentially would have to pee right next to each other without privacy. Awkward. Normally I would not be so apt to share a private moment with someone I had just met and was trying to impress. However, the few drinks I had consumed increased my boldness, and I simply asked Debra Sue if she wanted to use the bathroom at the same time. Having been at this restaurant many times and knowing the setup of the bathroom, she didn't hesitate in answering yes to sharing.

Dave's parents arrived the following morning, and the six of us explored the island, following Debra Sue and John's lead, as it was a place they visited often throughout the summer. While the rainy weather on Saturday forced us inside to stores and wineries, on Sunday the sun peeked out, and we hiked at the state park. Debra Sue remembers being relieved that I enjoyed being outside and active. I remember remarking to my mom in our next conversation that it was a fun weekend and I felt welcome, but that I could tell Debra Sue clearly took the lead when there was any indecision.

I was used to letting an older sister lead. While I was capable of leading, I had learned in my role of youngest child that Deb always had first choice to be in charge. Only if she willingly declined the role did I have the opportunity. I sensed that my position in Dave's family would be very similar.

Our relationship developed and cemented over the next several years. Debra Sue was my guardian on my first trip to meet the aunts, uncles, and cousins in Iowa. Speaking in her trademark Krenk frankness, she advised me of what to expect at each gathering. While Dave and I dreamed about details of our wedding, Debra Sue fawned over her cousin's infant. I was newly engaged, and my focus was all things white and flowery; Debra Sue had married soon after college graduation, and now, approaching their ten-year anniversary, she was ready for children. Though it was a time when we could have easily found ourselves at odds due to different seasons of life, we managed to stay engaged with each other and excited for new developments.

In the small window of time after our engagement and before Debra Sue's first child, Hunter, arrived, we enjoyed more time together. The two-and-a-half-hour trip was easier to fit into our schedules, and our lifestyles accommodated restaurants, bars, and weekend trips to remote islands.

One weekend we met on Pelee Island on the west side of Lake Erie. Through his fishing connections, John and Debra Sue had been invited to a fundraiser at the island's winery. When they extended us an invitation to join them, Dave and I were intrigued. We would need to travel to Windsor, Ontario, in order to ferry over to the island. Stormy weather on Friday evening resulted in the ferry being cancelled. Although we were less than an hour from home, Dave and I opted to rent a room at a local bed-and-breakfast in order to secure our spots on the first ferry in the morning. The sun shone and warmed the temperatures nicely for the remainder of the weekend. We rode our bikes everywhere, since there was no need for a car on the small island.

Being the only wine connoisseur of our group, Debra Sue chose a variety of wines for us to sample that evening. Never being much of a wine drinker, I was shocked at the intensity of the headache I had the next morning. Sleeping on John's boat with the constant rocking probably contributed to my overall sense of fatigue and shakiness. I gallantly tried to cover my distress as we began our adventures for the day. The first stop was breakfast at the small marina restaurant. While I assume all the food was tasty, only the smooth, sweet butter remains in my memory bank. Debra Sue recalled the bacon being the "best tasting ever."

Since John needed to move his boat and we had a few hours before Dave and I were to catch the return ferry, we loaded up and went for a ride around the island. At some point we anchored, and I perched myself on the stool to the left of the captain's chair. The movement of the boat, quiet conversation, and warm sun streaming in resulted in me falling asleep with my head rested on the cabin window. Debra Sue and John watched in amazement while I slept with my head moving up and down with the waves and occasionally banging on the plastic of the window. Dave was unimpressed, "Jo can sleep anywhere," he told them.

Debra Sue, an artist and elementary art teacher, offered me an education in noticing the details of life. Her detailed eye was especially useful while consignment shopping. I needed formulas and mannequins as examples. She seemed to be able to peruse the half-mile-long racks of used clothes and piece together classic and stylish outfits. She says that I am completely capable of this, too. Her purpose was really to boost my confidence by affirming choices I made with her guidance.

After children entered the picture for both of us—four total, two boys each in three years—our time together not only dwindled but was rarely spent with just the two of us. Caught in the windstorm of meals, naps, dressing, and changing diapers over and over again, we found little connection time. We never bemoaned our responsibilities, but they affected our relationship.

Then one spring Dave was out of town for five days to participate in a mountain bike race with friends in California. At the time, the TV show *While You Were Out* was popular. On the show a spouse or friend is lured away for forty-eight hours while a team of designers and craftsmen redo a room in the house. A few weeks before Dave left, I asked Debra Sue to come and help me pull a *While You Were Out* on Dave. Our mission was the master bedroom. Besides installing new carpet, we had not touched it since moving in two years earlier. The only direction I offered was a beach theme. Debra Sue arrived with all her design and artistic talent, along with paint samples and pictures, and guided me in finalizing a plan. With my two boys and her youngest, Wyatt, safely cordoned off in the house with a babysitter, we painted, accessorized, and distressed dressers (I distressed the furniture, and it's still not right). While paint was drying, we headed to Target to buy table lamps, which I learned must be in pairs. Gathering the kids to pile into my van, I realized that Debra Sue had taken the time to change out of her work clothes. She noticed that I had remained in my painting clothes. She asked what I would do if I saw someone I knew, and I responded that they would know I was painting.

While busy redecorating the room, we also had refreshingly deep conversations sharing the details of our stories closest to our hearts. There was plenty of laughter and a mutual sigh of relief as I admired her design knowledge and artistic eye, while she appreciated that I liked to paint ceilings.

It would seem that Debra Sue would have been the obvious choice to fill the gaping hole my sister's death left in my heart. She was my sister-in-law, and she didn't have a biological sister. She tells me that she was excited to have a sister in her family. On John's side she had a solid relationship with his two sisters but felt this would be different. While our early relationship seemed strong and on solid ground, a shift occurred later when I inadvertently caused a division of which I would not realize or understand the consequences of for years. We became very careful with our words, both afraid to say something that would anger the other. In any relationship, when you don't invest time, distance increases. While physical distance was certainly a factor, add in kids and their activities, and our shared time eroded away.

I wish I could remember what led to me banging my head (dramatically yet gently) on the table in my women's group as they unanimously agreed that I needed to offer an apology to Debra Sue. I had been burdened for far too long, and I knew it was causing me to close myself off to her. As I explained the situation, which has since been overshadowed by the memory of my reluctance, every single lady in the room agreed without hesitation that I needed to apologize for holding a grudge and letting it affect our relationship.

My suspicion that Debra Sue was unaware of any issue between us was confirmed when I approached her during a holiday weekend at her parents. Innocently enjoying a magazine and a moment of quiet in a house buzzing with four young boys, she was surprised by my apology. After listening to my admission of harboring resentment, she asked what she had done or said to upset me. I explained that I didn't feel that was the real issue and did not want to share it and therefore be distracted from my intended mission. At the time I thought I was helping our relationship by doing this. I have since learned that my lack of full disclosure created a chasm that remains to this day. Debra Sue explained later that she always felt I was a very private person, but after this admittedly mishandled apology, she was more cautious about the relationship. The revelation of this cautiousness was a lightbulb moment for me. I was well aware of my habit of measuring my words and thoughts around her yet could not identify the invisible boundary that surrounded Debra Sue. Enlightenment brought relief and also remorse that my apology—intended for reconciliation—had actually created further discord.

While Deb was alive, her personality overlapped with Debra Sue's in a way that I couldn't put words to, and it weighed me down and caused an additional awkwardness in how I related to Debra Sue. I found it hard to manage the similarities of a known sisterhood and a getting-to-know sisterhood. For the short time that Deb lived more than a day's drive away, I came to rely on Debra Sue in the mentor role that Deb had played for my entire life. Then Deb moved back only twenty minutes away, and I struggled to juggle these relationships yet again. After she died, it was an easy transference back to Debra Sue, except that now any reliance on Debra Sue felt like a betrayal of Deb as I became hyper vigilant to honor memories of my sister. A lifetime of admiring, following, and appreciating a sister does not evaporate upon her death. There was a huge hole where my sister used to be. Deb influenced my choices from an early age by tossing books into my crib, accompanying me to a neighborhood park, and later explaining algebra to me. I can still envision the swoops and swirls of her writing on the first page of a notebook she mailed to me celebrating my engagement to Dave. Her note explained how she had organized wedding information in a similar notebook and expressed her sincere excitement for our marriage. Deb was a lifelong mentor.

While Deb and Debra Sue enjoyed each other's company, they did not have many opportunities to visit. That did not dampen the shock when Debra Sue heard the news of Deb's death. Debra Sue remembers relating the details to her girlfriends while out for her birthday just a few days later and feeling shaken, like the situation was surreal. The day of the funeral, she and John drove in to offer their support. Debra Sue remembers my demeanor as calm, "just like always." As my family splintered after the luncheon, with no intention of being together, Debra Sue asked me if I wanted them to stay around. I acknowledged that they probably needed to get home to their boys, but with rare boldness I said it would be comforting to have them and my in-laws come back to our house. It was important for me to be surrounded by love that afternoon. We sat in chairs, on the couch, and on the floor while we chatted and actually laughed on occasion. Debra Sue's offer to visit with us longer meant so much to me. I wonder if our relationship would have deepened at this juncture if there hadn't been hundreds of miles between us. Or perhaps the miles protected her from my misplaced desire of replacing Deb that would have been unhealthy.

My admiration for Debra Sue drives how I relate to her. She is a strong leader, an influential teacher, and an artist. Debra Sue is independent and does not need a little sister to admire her and be devoted to her. Maybe Deb didn't need that either, but she learned to live with it—with me. Oddly enough, after our interview and the acknowledgment of cautiousness between us, I felt more bonded to Debra Sue. The strain that had blanketed our relationship was pulled back, and light filtered in. Perhaps a needed harmony was reached. Although filling a similar role in my life, I have learned that Debra Sue could not replace Deb.

# Chocolate Refrigerator Cookies

Deb insisted that we make these on our baking day every Christmas. I was never a fan of them, but I dutifully participated because it made her happy. I would do the same for Brandy.

| 1¼ cup butter, softened | 1½ cups confectioners' sugar |
|---|---|
| 1 egg | 3 cups flour |
| ½ cup cocoa | ¼ tsp. salt |
| 1½ cups nuts | |

Preheat oven to 400°F. Mix butter, sugar, and egg. Blend in flour, cocoa, and salt. Shape into two-by-eight-inch rolls; wrap the rolls in wax paper, seal the paper tightly, and chill the rolls for one hour. Slice in quarter-inch slices and bake for eight minutes.

# BRANDY

*The best friendships are built on a solid foundation of silliness, shenanigans and general misbehavior.*
—Unknown

Toenails and fingernails were shimmering with fresh color, salads were set before us, and our afternoon of pampering was coming to a close. Careful to keep the nail surface clear of dangers that might wreck the color, we lifted our forks and napkins daintily as if attending high tea. This was an afternoon to celebrate one of Brandy's milestone birthdays. I was eighteen months late in arranging it.

My brother's wife, Brandy, has always seemed younger than her real age—not immature, but youthful. One summer day I asked my brother what he was planning for Brandy's fortieth birthday the following March. A knowing smile eclipsed his face as he informed me that this birthday had already been celebrated the previous March. I, the person who holds birthdays in high regard, had messed up. Ugh. He also revealed that neither he nor her friends had done anything extraordinary to celebrate this occasion. Ugh. My mind began planning immediately.

As I processed out loud about arranging a pampering day, my brother cautiously confided in me that Brandy may not be interested in spending time with me. I was taken aback. I had thought we got along well and had fun together. He attempted to explain her feelings, and although hurt and sad, I resolved to respect them and not push.

The sticky issue became that it was my brother who told me Brandy's feelings. Possibly he wasn't 100 percent on target. He had been in an accident that caused a traumatic brain injury, which resulted in loss of short-term memory. So it was likely that he might have mixed up information, and more importantly he may not have remembered to tell Brandy what he shared with me. So I felt trapped. I couldn't approach Brandy to work it out, because she might be blindsided by the conversation. Although he intended to be helpful, what my brother shared left me sad and confused.

I decided to give Brandy space so our already infrequent communication became stretched even further apart. When we did communicate I forced myself to scale my enthusiasm down a notch, to listen instead of advise, to encourage, and to refrain from suggestions. In a subtle way, I intended to show Brandy that I valued our relationship and was willing to back off and engage at her level of comfort. I refused to travel a path that was well worn from years of escapes. I all too often gave up on people and relationships. Brandy was woven into my life so solidly that I was hard pressed to remember a time she wasn't part of our family. In conversation, I would mention a memory from my wedding expecting Brandy to recall it as well. Instead I am surprised by her blank stare because she wasn't there. She had filled my need for the fun parts of Deb—the carefree, passionate, bounds-of-energy parts of Deb I missed. I felt distraught at the thought that I might lose that.

In the following eighteen months, Brandy and I found ourselves at the usual family events: birthdays, holidays, and their move to a new home. Brandy never seemed distant and was always welcoming. The subject never arose until we were eating our salads.

I appreciated how she marched right into it. "There is something we need to talk about," she said.

I didn't want to assume, so I held up a mental stop sign to my thoughts, which already wanted to race ahead and solve the problem. And I listened. And it was good. She explained how the strengths she identified in me were areas she considered her weaknesses. She didn't feel bothered by me; instead, she was aware of character qualities in me that forced a self-evaluation. I was intrigued listening to her list of qualities she admired in me. Verbalizing traits I knew to be accurate but had never spent time naming myself, Brandy enlightened me.

What also struck me was that for every quality she could list about me, I could list traits I admired about her. In so many ways, I wished I had a pinch more of Brandy stirred in with my personality. Where I am composed, she is passionate. I share too little because I think the listener isn't really interested; she shares and draws the listener in. If you could blend our strengths, the result would be powerful.

It is impossible to be at a large event or intimate gathering and miss Brandy. Her personality is vivacious and her laugh engaging. When she tells a story, everyone is riveted. The party travels with her, and she never disappoints.

This wasn't my impression the very first time we met. Stu brought her to my mom's to celebrate Deb's birthday which, of course, included a double chocolate cake. As we gathered around the small round kitchen table to sing, Brandy seemed a bit reserved.

Shortly thereafter we kids left my mom's to attend the Michigan State Fair, a tradition from when my dad was alive; each year, near Deb's birthday, he would take us to the fair. This first year that Deb and Clayton were back in Michigan, we decided to revive the tradition. We drove in three separate vehicles, because we live in Motown and that's what we do, and separated while parking.

When Dave and I finally reached the ticket line, only Stu and Brandy were there. We chatted, and my inquisitive nature sprinkled the conversation with questions about Brandy's life. Unfortunately for her, Dave and I also had an agenda. We had planned to use this time to announce our pregnancy to Stuart. So while I was interested in finding out more about her, I was also anxious to share the exciting news. When there was a lull in the conversation, I made the announcement. Brandy handled it with grace and enthusiasm, although I can only imagine that it must have been a bit awkward. She has been an important part of my life ever since.

I grew up with the tradition of baking dozens upon dozens of cookies at Christmastime. My grandmother (Mom's mom) was a prolific baker. Around

Thanksgiving my grandmother would begin baking. Her basement kitchen was command central for all things sweet and fragrant. I have no idea who the recipients of all this baking were, but in a few flour-filled weeks, she would have a multitude of cookie tins stacked four and five high across twelve feet of tables in her basement.

Deb and I started baking with my grandma, as did the rest of my cousins, when we were quite young. One of Grammies favorite stories involved Deb and I decorating cutout cookies. We must have been preschool age, situated around the homemade cooling table my grandfather had fashioned from a card table. We were to use one teaspoon of a colored sugar to top the cutout cookies. Well, we decided that one teaspoon of *each* colored sugar would be much prettier. The end result was a heaping pile of sugar with a bit of cookie underneath.

Every year all the female relatives who were available would converge at my grandmother's to have a cookie day. We would help make a variety of cookies all day, and then, while the last batch was still cooling, we each were given a tin and were allowed to fill it from the stacks. Melt-in-your-mouth pecan balls, delicate pacer wafers (still a family favorite), traditional Scotch shortbread, simple cut-outs…the choices seemed endless.

The time we spent together baking on those days was filled with laughter and stories. It was a favorite event for me, even into my college years. Eventually, due to dementia, my grandmother had to be moved to a care facility, and a short time later she went home to be with Jesus. During that time cookie day ended as a group project, and everyone baked far less—at their own pace, in their own homes. My sister and mom had both moved out of state, so I carried on the tradition of cookie day solo.

Several years later, when we were all back in Michigan, we started gathering for cookie day again. We didn't make nearly the quantity or variety that my grandmother had, but we produced enough that each of us could take home large storage containers of sweets. We each picked our top choice to make, and each person brought a new recipe to try. Again, pecan balls, pacer wafers, and Scotch shortbread were headliners.

Looking back, it seems such a short few years before that all ended again. Deb and I had definitely caught the baking bug. Neither of us were afraid to experiment with recipes or try new ones. The first Christmas after Deb died, it was too difficult to even try to have a cookie day. But I missed it. The reality of grief settled in—the realization that many parts of my life would never be the same.

At some point I tried to revive cookie day. Quietly, I suggested to my cousins that they could come over and bake with me. That never caught on. Then as life evolved and twisted and I became closer to Brandy, I invited her to participate in cookie day, which at this point was just me with a little help from my boys. She seemed genuinely interested; however, her schedule was too full with all the events she already had planned with her sister and mom. They had their established family traditions and expectations. It would be stressful to fit in another person's traditions. Standing in Brandy's crowded kitchen while we prepared for her son's birthday party, I watched the interaction between her and her sister and felt the sting of realization that as much as I thought she could replace Deb, she already had a sister.

As our lunch continued that day, we laughed, cried, and laughed more. In the parking lot we hugged, and I told her how much I appreciated her courage to have that conversation. Sister relationships are fragile and can be volatile. Many times one sister is left wanting more than the other sister has the capacity to give. In sisters, God has given us the greatest capacity to love, forgive, and find pleasure in life. Through choices and personalities, this special relationship can also disappoint us or leave us lonely. While Brandy lives this truth with her own sister, I am envious that she has a sister to struggle and rejoice with. I want to have that role in Brandy's life. I miss the closeness, the inside jokes, and even the fighting. I know that Brandy loves and appreciates me, and I have learned to cherish what we have.

# Chocolate Mousse

This dish is simple, yet elegant. I imagine Karen serving this at one of her Oscar parties. Deb collected this recipe while in college and living on the ground floor of a house. In the small galley kitchen, she enjoyed tackling new recipes.

| | |
|---|---|
| ½ lb. semisweet chocolate | 5 eggs, separated |
| ½ oz. unsweetened chocolate | ¼ cup plus 1 tbsp. sugar |
| ¼ lb. butter, soft | 3 tbsp. orange liqueur |

Melt chocolate in double boiler. Remove from heat and beat in butter a little at a time until smooth. Beat yolks and ¼ cup sugar until mixture is pale yellow. Blend in liqueur. Continue to beat until it is the consistency of sour cream. Beat chocolate into egg mixture. Beat egg whites and a pinch of salt until soft peaks form. Add remaining sugar and beat until stiff. Fold beaten egg whites into chocolate mixture gently but thoroughly. Pour into dessert glasses and chill for six to eight hours.

## Karen C.

*We long to find someone who has been where we've been, who shares our fragile skies, who sees our sunsets with the same shades of blue.*
—Beth Moore

We sat in the dark wood booth with high backs that offered a bit of privacy. The sun was shining, but the window shades saved us from a blinding glare. Karen had chosen this restaurant because it was, in her words, "super casual, big variety, and they don't mind if you hang out for a while." Our substantial menus had not been cracked the first time the waitress asked if we were ready to order. Consumed by our conversation, neither of us looked past the second page for a selection. Our salads arrived accompanied by syrupy, calorie-laden dressings and pita bread that remained untouched.

Our friendship is one that survives long pauses, like a book you set aside and reopen to be immediately captivated again. Tragedy—the loss of a sister—binds us in a Celtic knot, a commonality we would trade readily, while appreciating how tough it is to be the survivor. Always, always, always, tears pool in my eyes as we gingerly tread into that sacred space of heartbreak.

Simon was still a baby, we had moved into our second home, and I desired stimulation beyond my parenting role. Over the previous year, I had attended multiple home parties for the same company with the same consultant. After three or four, I am sure Lynn suspected that there was an opportunity to have me join her team. I knew that it had to be in my timing. All the parties now combine in my memory and it is unclear which the first was and which was the one when I decided it was time to join the company. I do remember when I finally said yes to joining her team, Lynn remarking that she knew I would join eventually.

Having a focus other than my kids and cleaning the house was a much-needed distraction for me. Earning income and the incentive trips were a nice bonus, as well. In truth, it is unclear how much income I actually earned, since I am not a very astute businesswoman, and I only earned one incentive trip. That trip impacted me in many ways and provided a sense of accomplishment that I did not receive from my daily duties managing our family. However, there was one benefit from joining this organization that surprised me: friendship.

The first team meeting I attended was in a Jewish cultural center. Each team leader hosted her own table populated with her team and their guests. The room was loud due to conversation and dark due to dim lighting. Fun and purpose filled the agenda. Games were interspersed with talks from experienced and brand-new team members. I assume that I followed my normal mode of operation to engage minimally, so I could quietly observe the vast array of personalities: the outgoing, loud no-filter types that get the most attention; the quiet, observant note-takers who leave unnoticed; the welcoming, smiling, gatherers of people who make sure no one is left out; and the detail-oriented information seekers who shush everyone speaking out of turn. While spacious physically, the room was packed with personality. The experience was overwhelming and exciting. Of course, leaving that meeting I did not know that my sister would be murdered in a few months and how God would intertwine my life with the life of one of these women.

It seems shameful that I don't recall how Karen and I met. Besides being confident that it was through this company, since we were on the same team, I cannot remember the circumstances of our initial encounter. So I asked Karen.

"Here's what I remember: We were both doing Discovery Toys under Lynn, and she kept talking about you. I just kept hearing your name, but I'd never met you. People kept saying things like, 'Well, you know Joanna…' And I was like, 'No!' Lynn even said she thought we would get along really well. And then I remember sitting on Lynn's couch, and you were nearby on the floor and someone called your name and I was like "Finally! I'll get to meet Joanna!" And I think after the meeting or whatever you came over and introduced yourself. The rest is history."

I have always been drawn to Karen's thoughtful responses. They are slow and methodical, and she never interrupts. The twinkle of deviousness I see on occasion reminds me of Deb. Sometimes the twinkle happens when we are dreaming: "Hmm, how could we make this happen?"

One evening we met at a coffee shop. Karen had been in possession of my manuscript for *shoo g-er* for a while, and I was anxious to hear her thoughts. She paged through the six-inch pile of paper systematically, always keeping her remarks positive while guiding me to improve the work. She kept repeating, "I like this story, but there must be more to it." And I would respond, "Oh yes, that is the funniest story." Her eyes would widen, and a smile grew as she nodded and said, "We want to hear it." She helped me break out of the shell I had been in most of my life. As the youngest in our home, I grew up with a sense—an unsaid understanding—that my opinion wasn't valuable. What I had to say or share was of little importance. No one was interested. Therefore my writing was stale. My stories didn't entertain or convey the magnitude of the effect situations had on me. Karen, with a twinkle in her eye, convinced me that the details were important and people cared. She cared.

We all perceive ourselves differently than others see us. Our own worst critics, we heap on the negative thoughts. In a friendship it is rare to speak of the specific role each person assumes. From the time our friendship was like a fledgling bird, tipping over the edge of the nest and awkwardly flapping its wings to fly for the first time, Karen always presented herself confident and secure. Never did I see a sliver of insecurity. So when she opened up about her lifelong search for a best friend, my mind perked up with interest. Karen shared how she always felt second best, second fiddle, not quite enough as a friend. Her remarks stirred in me a similar sentiment, an underlying thread that no one said out loud but you sense is true. Deb was always favored. There, I said it. In my nuclear family I lived in the shadow of my sister, with brief breaks of sunlight cast on me.

I understood Karen's feeling while also disagreeing with her assessment. For I transposed my own feeling of inadequacy on our friendship. With her wisdom, humor, and creativity, she clearly had more to bring to the table. While Karen felt "lied to by the world" because in all the TV shows female characters had best friends, I suffered from wanting everyone to like me. So we both had walls to protect us from eventual disappointment. Through consistent interactions that increased our trust in each other, we dismantled the walls.

The business that allowed us to meet became a dividing point in a few years. I was focused on growing my business and earning an incentive trip, and apparently this dominated my conversations. In the same season, Karen was pregnant with her third child and winding her business down. The common thread between us was disappearing. For a time there was radio silence as we embraced our futures. Thankfully our friendship was deeply rooted and survived this period. We had the opportunity to reconnect at a park near her house one summer day. The boys and I were spending the day with my nephew, and she had her youngest with her. While they played, we reminisced, shared parenting challenges, and caught up on life. It seemed as if no time had separated us. A common sentiment shared then and many times over the years was, "I wish we lived closer."

Not long after that day, Karen's sister, Donna, would begin her final journey with cancer. Donna was already a survivor, and now her cancer had returned. Karen admitted that when I lost Deb abruptly, she had no idea how to respond to me. When Karen shared that her sister's cancer was terminal, I felt a similar sense of helplessness for my friend. There is not a "better way" to lose a sister. It always hurts and the sting never dulls.

I attended Donna's funeral on a wintry day. I arrived just minutes before the service began and quickly sat in the first seat I found near the back of the large sanctuary. Reminiscent of Deb's funeral, the place was overflowing with people who loved Donna. Following the touching service, Karen left with her family before I had the opportunity to give her a hug. It was important to me that she knew I had come to support her, so I texted her how heartfelt the service was. Years later she still laments that we didn't get to talk that day.

While Christ is the center of our lives and our friendship now, He was not always. Karen admitted to being stagnant in her faith when we met. To my newbie Christian ears, some of her words sounded like she knew Jesus, while I am sure many of my words and actions were quite contrary to Christian beliefs. So we danced around the subject for a time, until, as Karen puts it, it just came out and our friendship allowed us to grow together in our faith.

Over time we both grew a heart for missions, something I never expected for myself. While I have yet to journey to a foreign country on a mission trip, Karen, who travels for pleasure regularly, blended faith and pleasure and landed in North Africa. I was excited for her to go and then to connect with her upon her return. Circumstances would have it that our homeschool writing group was studying North Africa in the same time frame. So Karen, because she is amazing, came to our group and shared with the kids some cultural insights, the dangers of the area, and the beauty of the people. We prepared traditional North African and southern Spanish delicacies while Karen treated us all to Moroccan mint green tea, served in an authentic kettle and cups.

Observing Karen parent her three kids over the years, I can picture Deb. Karen's patience mixed with a sarcastic sense of humor is how I imagine my sister would have been as a mom. Certainly the tolerance for ever-changing hair color and the newest expression of one's personality through clothes and music are areas where Karen allows—and I like to assume Deb would have allowed—much freedom. Maybe because she had to suppress her own rebellion so that she would fit in, Karen now encourages her kids to express themselves.

Karen is an avid reader like Deb, and I wonder if reading was an outlet for her squelched adventuresome spirit until she had the resources and courage to live out real-life adventures.

While I revel in the nostalgia of Deb that I experience being with Karen, I realize that it doesn't fill the hole permanently. Regardless, watching her life on Facebook and enjoying our occasional talks and infrequent visits remind me that some people are attached for life. I can't imagine that we will ever mention our sisters without tears welling in our eyes, and I am grateful to have a girlfriend who understands.

# Malt-Whisky Truffles

A surprising mix of delicate and rough, the malt whisky gives these little balls a kick. This page from my sister's book, *The Cook's Guide to Chocolate,* is marked with a yellow sticky tab that causes me to wonder what caught her attention in this recipe? It reminds me of Monica and me, ourselves a surprising mix of delicate and rough.

| 7 oz. dark chocolate, chopped | 3 tbsp. malt whisky |
|---|---|
| ⅔ cup double cream | ¾ cup confectioners' sugar |

Melt the chocolate in a heatproof bowl over a saucepan of simmering water. Stir until smooth and then allow to cool slightly. Using a wire whisk, whip the cream with the whisky in a bowl until thick enough to hold its shape. Stir in the melted chocolate and confectioners' sugar, mixing evenly, and then leave until firm enough to handle. Dust your hands with cocoa powder and shape the mixture into bite-size balls. Store in the refrigerator for up to three or four days.

# Monica

*Two persons cannot long be friends if they cannot forgive each other's little failings.*
—Jean de la Bruyere

The conversation began the day before in texts:

Me: Are you busy after study on Tues? I need to interview you for my book. :)

Monica: Uhmmm…is it to give an example on how not to train and take care of your body?! Lol I am intensely curious, so yes. Want to have lunch at church or ?

Me: At church, love the cafe. So you can prep. I am writing about our friendship. So what is your first memory of meeting me, significant other experiences together, how did I tell you about Deb dying and anything else that comes up :)

Monica: Hmmm…all right. That could get raw real quick ;)

Me: Good :)

Monica: Ha! Already running it through my mind and starting to tear up…

Me: I'll bring tissue (heart)

This is us: Bible study, being real, teasing, love, and too many smiley face emojis. We agreed in our conversation that day that our time together has never comprised of the traditional fun of girls' weekends, mani-pedis, or dancing and drinking. Our friendship is defined by a different kind of fun: meaningful experiences, accountability, and growth.

We settled in at a round, high table just outside the cafe with our salads and my sweet potato fries. As we expected it would, the conversation quickly exposed raw emotions. After an hour or so, I teared up. It wasn't unexpected, since I often do. Monica laid her hand on my arm as I took a few seconds to gain enough composure to talk again. Our conversation had covered a lot of history so far, and she had firmly yet softly told me about some personality traits of mine that made her bristle. We had covered so much life together that she felt burdened to speak frankly about my difficult yet true character flaws. In a flash her honesty caused me to intensely miss Deb again.

As I reviewed my notes later, I could picture my sister having this raw conversation with me. She would have been honest in telling me that I rationalize rules and that it irritated her. My sister, like Monica, would have pointed out how that tendency is steeped in pride and inconsistency, and she would have done it just like Monica: with tenderness and love. In delving deeper into our friendship, this conversation revived a longing for the honesty I shared with Deb.

Monica and I met when our boys were little, at a meeting for moms where we were randomly placed in the same group. Her oldest son and my youngest, we would discover, were only two weeks apart in age. The focus of our group—fittingly called Mentoring Moms—was to learn and grow together as mothers. There were eight to ten other moms around the table. The one identified as the leader was a step ahead of us on the parenting journey.

It was providence that Monica and I connected with each other. It was the first group environment at church that either of us had waded into, and Monica shared with me, years later that she was scared and felt as though she didn't belong, though she also felt she needed to be there. She sensed that I felt the same way. She was correct. As wonderful and warm as our leader, Susan, was, it was tough. We had only been attending church for a year or so, and I had no idea what to expect. Would I have to stand up and read from the Bible? (I didn't.) Was there an expectation that I could quote Bible verses from memory? (There wasn't.) What if women were mean? (They weren't.) We returned each week, grew as mothers, developed skills, and bonded.

Monica later explained our blossoming friendship: "You felt safe to me, someone I felt comfortable with."

As it happened we were at the same table for the group's second semester; a study about love languages. I was astonished to find out that my most prominent love language was gifts. That language seemed very materialistic, and I did not consider myself materialistic. I wanted another one. Physical touch sounded intriguing. Like most women, I assumed that was predominately a male gift. Stereotypically, they always wanted to be touched, right? However, as we began delving deeper into the qualities of each gift, there was an aspect of physical touch that seemed to strike a chord with me—and with Monica, too, I learned through table conversation. The study explained that physical touch is not just human-to-human interaction; it also includes a physical response to the Holy Spirit. One way a person might respond physically is by raising a hand while listening to worship music. I had often fought the urge to raise my hands, instead tapping my foot or moving my legs to the rhythm. During that discussion Monica and I both shared that we would enjoy breaking free from our self-conscience prison and worshipping freely.

Years later we found ourselves sitting in the same row for a church service. Our families were distributed to the right and left of us while we worshipped without restraint or concern.

Monica told me after the service, "I just had this thought of, man, we have come far in our spiritual journey! And it was just so beautiful to me that we were standing together worshiping the Lord together in that way when I knew that it had been a struggle for both of us to get there." Monica's memory of that time conveyed our brand of fun.

Also, we both served in our kids' ministry at church, and we sat next to each other at a seminar for the volunteers. I was already seated when Monica walked in. I noticed her as she slid into the same row a few feet from me. Our eyes met and brightened as recognition dawned on her. After our initial greeting, I acknowledged that perhaps God kept drawing us together. Unknown to the other, we both were working through some tough issues in our lives. During this seminar we were asked to share our hurts with a neighbor. After sharing we completed an exercise that involved a Band-Aid. While I don't remember the exact purpose of the bandage, I remember the vulnerability in our voices as Monica and

I shared our hurts with each other. The Band-Aid remained in my purse for years as a token of the day the roots of our friendship dug solidly into the ground.

Our connection might have seemed convenient due to the connection of our boys. They played well together and shared a similar adventurous spirit. Through the years, they spent many Tuesday mornings together in class while Monica and I deepened our faith and grew our friendship during our women's group.

After two semesters with Mentoring Moms, we bravely moved into a women's Bible study. The name alone was intimidating because I had never studied the Bible. All the fears from Mentoring Moms resurfaced. I no longer had the security of Monica's presence, since we did not know that we could request to be in the same group. I survived and met new friends, and in the next session we were reunited at our request. Our new group was comprised of women from a variety of backgrounds and various seasons of life, but we melded quickly.

It was from this group that we first called ourselves the "old ladies." These women, who were and are still not old, traversed many highs and lows, thrills and heartbreaks, and celebrations and quietness with us. Although over the course of the years we would see some ladies come and go, our core group remained the same through a variety of studies. Our official group leader was Millie. After several seasons of studies, she no longer allowed us to let her shoulder all the responsibility. Like every great leader, she forced us to participate at a higher level, which eventually moved us all to lead groups ourselves. This is when we dubbed ourselves the "old ladies," not describing age or attitude but simply referring to our previous grouping, not to be confused with the ladies in the groups we were currently leading. In addition to Monica, Millie, and me, there was Pam, Cindy, Diane, Lynne, AnnJanette, Kayla, Karen, Sue, and Suzi. We discussed, supported, simplified, and lived life together for many seasons. Monica describes the group this way: "A group of women who wanted to seek God, all stumbling in some way. But we chose Him, and we chose Him together."

When we each felt the nudge to lead different groups, our time together became scarce. While we would meet as a group several times a year to catch up, Monica's life and mine continued to intertwine more regularly. Both our families enjoyed camping, and for one weekend each summer we would "rough it" together with several other families. The friends' camping trip had originated several years earlier with a different conglomeration of families, transitioned to a new location with a different mix of families, mine and one other as the core. Monica's family wasn't in attendance the first year in this new location, but they joined us faithfully each subsequent year. We have watched our kids get dirty together, splash for hours in the lake, and toast marshmallows in the heat of the fire. It was not unusual or uncomfortable for Monica and me to sit quietly side by side at the lake or by the fire.

Each annual camping weekend seemed to produce a circumstance that became an entertaining story for future campfires. Rarely were they amusing in the moment, but over time we all shared a laugh about it. For Monica, there is the year we lost Sam, her youngest, energetic, and friendly child. He climbs like a monkey and loves his mama deeply. Since we all have campsites adjacent to each other, the kids move freely from one to the other while adult eyes keep a loose oversight on the group. Sam was the youngest of all the kids by several years, and he was sometimes left behind by the older kids.

One afternoon Monica's husband was in and out of his truck, and Sam was helping him by playing in the back seat. As Jeff finished with the truck, he closed the door, assuming Sam was off playing with the kids. Not too much later, Monica asked Jeff where Sam was. He didn't know. All the adults began searching, a bit unhurriedly to begin with because we assumed we would find him at one of our campsites. Within minutes the alert status raised as he remained missing. We searched the campground, bathrooms, and beach. As the park ranger drove by we asked him to keep an eye out for Sam. In these handful of minutes, Monica's mind whirled with a mother's worst fears and a building tension toward Jeff since he seemed responsible for Sam's disappearance.

After returning to their campsite several times, Monica finally heard Sam's cry from the back of the truck. She explained that every time she started searching elsewhere she felt drawn back to their campsite. He had still been playing in the backseat of the truck when Jeff closed the door. Monica opened the door, grabbed Sam, held him tight, and kissed him, which settled him down quickly. Monica, on the other hand, was visibly frazzled. As a mom, I understood the fear that had overwhelmed her. A natural reaction of lashing out was acceptable but not helpful. Realizing she needed time to settle down, I told her to take Sam to the playground. I joined her at the picnic table where she sat with tear stained cheeks. After a time of silent processing, I sensed she was ready to talk to Jeff. As she approached him, all the other men were talking with him, and their faces showed concern as she approached. She grabbed him and kissed him, and all was well again, while Sam cheerfully played with my watchful eye keeping him in view.

While all these memories paint an accurate picture, it is incomplete. Our families have different personalities. Mine always has an agenda and a purpose—yes, even while camping. Monica's is laid back and unstructured. And this is where the tension hits. We both share a common goal of harmony, but our tactics are as opposite as milk and dark chocolate taste. I attempt to gain consensus quietly; Monica lays it all out there without regard to the waves created. In my desire for everyone to be happy, I tend to set aside my own family's comfort. Monica remembers a time when our families shared a cabin. My boys wanted to sleep in the top bunks, but I wouldn't let them move into their desired bunks until all the families were there and everyone had a say in the sleeping arrangements. Unfortunately for my boys, I became irritated when they resisted my plan and expressed this to them by yelling. Monica overheard me which caused her to want the boys to just have the top bunks. Our mutual desire for harmony was at odds.

Another time when our families were spending the weekend together, I was unsettled for some reason, and Monica watched me wallow in it for a day. I couldn't identify the cause of my uneasiness, but she finally did.

"The boys are old enough that you don't have to manage them or their time," she told me.

Ah, that was it. She knew, and she cared enough to be frank with me. Although it may sound harsh, it was a gift. I would have spent the weekend agitated and most likely caused distress to others, especially Dave. Her accurate diagnosis allowed me to enjoy the weekend.

That is the cornerstone of our friendship: caring enough to hold each other accountable, guide the other, and be frank, all in love. When Monica gets irritated with me or there is a misunderstanding between us, bitterness doesn't grow because we know each other's hearts. Monica put it this way: "In spite of the distress, I know your heart. I love and trust you completely." My soul warmed at the revelation. For weeks I had battled an unseen enemy that sought to force a fissure in our relationship. There was a misunderstanding or perhaps a lack of communication, which led to a gap between what I anticipated and what Monica intended. An exchange of e-mails with the intention of providing information became twisted in my mind to be confrontational. Monica's tone in the e-mails surprised me, and since I can be sensitive, I took it personally.

The following weeks became a battle zone for my spirit over whether to withdraw or pursue the truth. My normal pattern was to withdraw, to throw in the towel, and to just plain give up. Instead, this time I took action. I knew her heart was not to hurt me, and honestly, she is so much tougher than I am that she probably didn't even realize how I struggled with her response. Our friendship would not become stagnant. Each time the thought crept in, I battled it by reminding myself, "That's not Monica."

After several weeks of this inner struggle, our families were together at a rental house to enjoy a few days at the beach. In a simple sweet moment as we passed while unloading our bags, she grabbed me into one of her famous bear hugs. My tension evaporated immediately. That is her heart.

Monica does admit that as much as my planning and agenda-based personality irritates her, it also comes in handy. Both our hearts are filled by serving, and it is a double blessing when we have the opportunity to serve together. However, God placed different burdens on our hearts. One of mine is providing access to clean water for communities in Africa, and my avenue for fundraising is to participate in endurance events. This is not the burden that God placed on Monica's heart, yet every fall she rises at 3:00 a.m. to join me in supporting our athletes at the marathon in Detroit. Her own burden is for struggling teen girls. From pregnancy to abuse to homelessness, their hardship is real and very foreign to me. As Monica dove deeper into mentoring girls in these situations, I longed to be burdened similarly. While God never established this burden in me, I was able to utilize my organizational skills to help Monica plan holiday parties for the girls living at a residential treatment home. Monica and I are both rooted in our desire to serve God and thankful when we can also help each other. This is our brand of fun.

The devotion I read yesterday morning from *Savor* by Shauna Niequist was on the topic of grace. I realized that grace is the foundation of my friendship with Monica, and it mirrors my relationship with Deb. Just like sisters, Monica and I go through times of tension, but those times are always followed by forgiveness and grace. As I continue to wander on this journey of missing part of my heart, God is gracious to patch in the holes with friends as meaningful as Monica.

# Viennese Torte

This rich, dense dessert was a delight to my taste buds in Vienna and a surprise to find in my sister's recipe box. Very much like meeting Ja and Lee.

| | |
|---|---|
| ½ package vanilla wafers (11 oz) | 2 eggs, separated |
| ⅓ cup ground walnuts | 1 pint sugared raspberries |
| ¼ cup melted butter | 1 cup heavy cream |
| ½ cup soft butter | 1 tbsp. confectioners' sugar |
| 1 cup confectioners' sugar | 8 oz. dark chocolate |

Blend vanilla wafers in a blender to make crumbs and mix with ground nuts. Add melted butter. Divide crumb mixture in half and use one half to line a buttered nine-inch springform pan for bottom crust. Set aside other half of mixture. Cream soft butter, add confectioners' sugar, and blend thoroughly. Add egg yolks one at a time to mixture and beat thoroughly. Beat the egg whites until stiff and fold into mixture. Spread this mixture over layer of crumbs in the pan. Arrange berries over surface of crust. Whip cream and sugar until peaks form. Cover berries with cream. Sprinkle remaining crumbs over top of whipped cream. Refrigerate overnight. Before serving melt dark chocolate in microwave with one teaspoon of coconut oil. Drizzle over individual slices of cake.

## JA & LEE

*If you will live like no one else, later you can live like no one else.*
—Dave Ramsey

I was backing out of the driveway when my phone flashed with a text from Lee. She was running a few minutes late. In her rush to help in her son's class before our meeting, she had left her purse at home. She would be on her way after retrieving it. Classic Lee—busy as a bee. Ja (pronounced "jay"), on the other hand, walked through the coffee house door as unhurried and put together as always. Her broad smile and engulfing hug followed her greeting of "Hey, girl!"

The barista, whose name is also Joanna, greets many people each day, and I wonder if she thinks we are quite the motley crew. Our appearances are wonderfully varied, and so are our beverage choices. My steaming cup holds green tea with a healthy dollop of honey. Ja waits a bit for her white chocolate mocha, since she had two cups of coffee at home, and Lee sips on a breve latte with no foam while enjoying a toasted everything bagel with cream cheese. I was concerned that the sound from the television over my left shoulder would distract me, but as we dove into our conversation, the sound of these voices—a sweet melody from times past—keeps me focused.

I stalk people. There, I admitted it. It's not often, and it's not creepy. When I notice a remarkable person and want to build a relationship with her, I figure out her habits, search out ways to connect with her, and then do it. The trouble is that she doesn't know yet that we would get along famously. Thus I have to observe them, perhaps leverage a common friend, and find a way to weasel into her life. I am not a parasite; it is my full intention to benefit her, as well.

Lee appeared on my radar first through her reputation for very successful parties in our organization. Due to the close relationship between her leader and mine, I was able to connect with her, and she graciously allowed me to observe her at a party. This party was a challenge, to put it lightly. The group of ladies liked to talk. And there were kids. Have I mentioned we sold toys? It was chaos. But Lee handled it masterfully. I was mesmerized at how she controlled the side conversations and effectively refocused the ladies several times throughout her demonstration. She seemed to not even notice the kids scattering her demonstration toys under couches and around the room. She was unflappable despite the distractions, and her friendly, bubbly personality endured. While I appreciated the important business tips I gleaned from observing Lee, I left the party with the desire to know her more. Little did I know then that our friendship would begin across the Atlantic Ocean.

Neither of us can remember the purpose for us being at the same business meeting, but we do remember that the host home was dark. Ja points out that the room was lit only with table lamps, which were the source of the dim lighting. I am not sure I could have identified Ja after the meeting, because the lighting kept us all in shadows, but her name was synonymous in my mind with accomplishment. She had joined our company and jumped right on the fast track. The rapid growth caused many other consultants to study her strategies and put them to use themselves. I knew I would see her in a few months on the incentive trip we had both earned.

The destination of the trip was Vienna, Austria. Several hundred consultants from our company had earned the twenty-fifth-anniversary trip. There was a reception on the first evening. Ja, her husband, Dan, and I sat at the same table and had a chance to chat. I will admit I was distracted. My mind was figuring my way into Lee's plans for later in the evening. Ja, on the other hand, told me later that this is when she felt secure on the trip. Until that first dinner, she was unsure whom she and her husband would hang out with. My stalking mode in full alert, I was able to snare the four of us an invitation to the post-reception activity. We walked with several couples to a club and enjoyed an evening of talking and observing local culture. Despite the loud music that caused us to yell in order to be heard, it was a blast.

That evening set the tone for the remainder of our trip. Our paths continued to cross whether we ended up on the same tour of a historical building, sipping hot chocolate at the hotel bar or exploring the city after dinner. One night we ventured to an Irish bar Dave and I had walked by earlier in the day. Our company had divided everyone on the trip into smaller groups for dinner that evening. Each group was assigned to a restaurant. Our group included almost everyone we knew on the trip. It would be the perfect mix of people to enjoy that Irish bar. Concerned the group would not readily follow me, after dinner I strolled up to Lee and Brad and mentioned the Irish bar as we walked away from the quaint restaurant. Thankfully it sounded interesting to them as well, so they rallied our traveling party.

"Do you speak English?" I asked the waiter as he approached the large oval table our party had secured.

"Yes, I am Irish," he replied in a very authentic brogue, sending us all into rolling laughter.

We stayed for hours, making new friends with the locals, discovering similarities, and filling the mostly empty establishment with laughter. Our roles in the new friendships came to light faster than they would have at home, but I also believe our bonds strengthened faster, as well. When you happen to be on the same tour of church catacombs and the only other Americans are people you "know," it's easy to call them friends. In fact, Ja told me later that it was in those cramped, centuries-old tunnels filled with centuries-old remains that she knew we could be friends.

Certainly there were other couples and families from our area on this trip, and we all enjoyed each other. In fact, I felt like the outsider on many occasions. A handful of the women were all on the same team and had an established connection. In a way I inserted myself into their established hierarchy. While that seems bold, both Ja and Lee tell me that the impression I left then, and still leave today, was of quietness and constant analysis. What they soon discovered was that when I become comfortable and especially when I am in a smaller group, my sarcasm and sense of humor are revealed.

Some friendships come in packages: while we are certainly friends separately, when I think of one person I always connect the second in no particular order. Ja and Lee are that way.

When I hang out with people I consider more fun, hip, and influential than I am, I feel inferior. I prepare myself for the time, which seems inevitable, when I am no longer included. What never occurred to me getting to know Ja and Lee is that either of these ladies might think more of me than I did.

After our Vienna trip, we committed to weekly calls with the purpose of building our businesses. For one hour per week we shared, encouraged, and equipped each other. Through our calls we discovered that Ja is not to be crossed (Lee said that, not me), the two of them are excellent entrepreneurs, and I could make us laugh. We developed a deep, lasting connection that ripened as we appreciated each other's strengths and accepted faults.

I sometimes envision the three of us written into the ending scene of *The Breakfast Club* (if you haven't seen this movie, you must) with Anthony Michael Hall's voice describing us: "In the simplest terms, in the most convenient definitions," we are busy (Lee), business minded (Ja), and controlled (me).

Another reason our friendship flourished is due to our husbands. They actually enjoyed each other as well. Not that they called each other or hung out without us (do men do that?), but whenever we made plans they didn't protest, and laughter abounded. While their interests varied, each one made an effort to include the others. All three couples were also walking through a similar season of life: young children, paying off debt, and finding our faith.

A central theme in each of our lives is that each couple had one spouse that had grown up Catholic. In most cases this would seem trivial, but we were all coming together at a time when faith was just beginning to take shape for each of us—a time when we wanted to raise our kids in faith, yet we were figuring out how that looked different from our own childhood experiences. Although I wouldn't realize it for months, I was the furthest along in my faith walk. We don't remember how the awareness happened, but fairly early in our friendship Lee and I could tell we were on the same journey while neither of us had a sense of where Ja stood.

One day when I visited her home, Ja and I had a defining moment. Her girls were little and well-behaved, so it was easy to have a conversation while they played. Ja was seated on a couch while I was across the room in a deep-brown, comfy chair. Like many conversations among women, we jumped from topic to topic and eventually landed on religion. When she married Dan, Ja had agreed that their family would be Catholic, though it was his religion, not hers. Attending mass was frustrating since she was occupied with the keeping the girls quiet in the pew. While they had attempted to find community, it proved difficult due to the culture of their parish. During my visit that day, Ja pinpointed her dissatisfaction. On our business-building calls, as Lee and I mentioned the different activities we participated in at our churches, she realized that community was what Lee and I had and she desired.

I invited her to attend a service with us, but she felt certain that Dan would never agree. However, her openness gave me boldness to keep asking. Next I invited her to a Christmas show at my church. Well known in the community as a Broadway-level production, Ja was interested, but her husband flat out refused to attend. The next invitation I extended was at Easter, which they did attend. Dan was amazed that in such a large church Ja already knew several people. Attending that Easter service was the catalyst for them to learn the difference Lee and I had already discovered between religion and relationship. It was an exciting privilege to share their faith journey.

Although our lives were increasingly woven together, there was a piece of my history that I kept neatly tucked away. I struggled with the feeling that my identity was tied too closely to Deb's murder. Desiring separation from that event swayed me in the opposite direction of never sharing that part of my story, so much so that when Ja and Lee learned of her death, they were both shocked.

"I hurt for you as I processed the information," Lee shared with me later. I had disclosed the news to her while we were at a retreat. She recalls sitting in a chair near a fireplace in the hotel lobby. As I shared the details she sank deeper into the chair only able to look into the flames of the fire.

Ja moved into a traditional colonial two miles from my home on a damp fall day. Our lives became intertwined like the branches of a clematis: stopping over, sitting together at church, attending the same small group, taking care of each other's kids, and volunteering at the same events. This way of life felt very natural and comfortable.

Three years into our friendship, a simple question from Ja created the opportunity to share the story with her. We sat at her newly purchased kitchen table, cups of tea in our hands, as I told of my sister's murder. Ja was disappointed in us both: in me for not sharing earlier and in herself for not asking. It wasn't my intention to hide this part of my story; however, it isn't the easiest story to share out of the blue over a hot cup of tea. Regardless, holding a secret is a wound to a friendship. I understood their feeling of betrayal as they both wondered how we could have been friends for so long without me sharing this piece of my story.

Then a cold snap hit our season of friendship. I was in the midst of coordinating a large, weeks-long collection effort at our church. During one of the most intense weeks, my oldest child was also getting baptized at our midweek service. My in-laws were traveling two hours to attend the baptism, and that morning I was notified that the time of the baptism was being moved two hours earlier. Now just one or two of those circumstances would have been manageable, but all of them whipped around in my brain like a tornado, and I broke. I called Ja to inform her of the change in baptism time, and as I spoke the stress revealed itself in my tears. She rallied like a good friend would and offered to fill in for me the following morning to manage the collection of shoe boxes. It was a welcomed relief that allowed me to regroup. Unfortunately, personalities clashed between her and another volunteer. I decided to let them resolve their issue without stepping into the middle of it. That caused awkwardness between Ja and me. Our friendship was already shifting to a new season, quite possibly due to the rapid growth in her new business. She was extremely busy networking and growing her business. As I saw her Facebook posts having lunch with one person and coffee with another, I felt left out. My role in her life was diminishing. I wondered if we had unsteadily transitioned into a new season of friendship where our paths didn't cross as often, or did we suffer a fissure? Although saddened and confused, I did nothing to redress the situation. I own that. Instead, I allowed time to quiet my emotions and settle me into our new season of friendship.

Lee was absent during this tumultuous time because she left us. Yep, that woman moved her family to Florida for four long years. When anyone moves to Florida from Michigan, the motivation is always questionable unless they outright admit to desiring more tolerable weather. Actually, I had a seed of jealousy toward Lee. They had decided to be a part of the launch team for the Florida campus of their church. To me that seemed exciting and adventurous, and it was Florida, for Pete's sake. Launching a church is no easy task, especially with a growing family. As with anything Lee does, she jumped right in to her transplanted life. We were able to visit once when they returned to Michigan one summer and a few years later when our family was in Florida. The distance alone could have caused our friendship to evaporate like water on pavement in the Florida sun, but thankfully through social media we were able to still feel involved in each other's life happenings. What the distance revealed was that the roots of our friendship were deep enough to survive the drought of distance.

While our friendship has been quite the adventure, it has stayed its course. We are different—dare I say better?—than we were in Vienna. Lee is back in Michigan, joyfully managing family, business, and travel, while Ja continues to exceed expectations in her company and keep her family grounded. I am writing, completely unexpectedly, and have narrowed my focus of volunteer roles. However, when I look back on our *Breakfast Club* ending, the descriptions still ring true. Positioned in my life at the exact right time, their personalities touched my life with the familiarity of Deb.

## Afterword

For those of you who have already enjoyed *shoo g-er*, you may be confused as to why my friends, Jessica and Robin, are not written about in this work. I would have expected them to be. Certainly they were ever present, supportive, and—well, I can't even sum up in words how important they were in the days, months, and years following Deb's death.

They weren't, oddly enough, recipients of my misplaced search for someone to replace Deb. I am confident it was part of God's protection. Perhaps I unconsciously already knew that with all their loveliness, neither of them was my sister. There was no point to include them in the search. Of course, I was fully cognizant of the depth of their characters and how special they were in my life. I hope you have at least one girlfriend like they were to me—one you know intimately, accept, and embrace who they are, and who does the same for you.

As God has developed me as a writer, I have learned to let stories unfold naturally and to have a loose plan and direction without forcing ideas. For instance, the chapter about Karen was originally written for *shoo g-er*, but in the end it didn't fit. I was very sad. I loved the emotions in that chapter. Then God showed me how it would nestle in with my other girlfriend stories much better. So as I wrote CHÖK'LIT, I focused on the friendships that God laid on my heart. My memory fails and my perception is narrow, so I fully rely on His perspective.

Those of you who know me now might be surprised that my current friends are not mentioned. Me too! Because I am surrounded by a variety of supportive and hilarious women who make life an adventure. Some I have known for several years, some for just a few seasons; with all of them, it feels like I have never known life without them. However, this book is about a specific time period in my life, and although it might seem my search was wide and broad, it wasn't. Few made the first cut in my search to replace Deb.

What might seem like an abrupt ending really wasn't. It was a gift that was presented at exactly the right time. Through God's timing, my heart was healing, although it will never be whole again. As my search became less intense and the feeling of loss consumed fewer and fewer moments in my days, my half-sister, Fran, reached out. She was placed for adoption at birth, and I had only known of her existence, nothing else. Meeting her and learning about her was the perfect conclusion to this season of searching. Fran did not replace any part of Deb, but she solidified for me the realization that no one ever would. And that is OK. Accepting this allowed me to open my spirit to the uniqueness and blessings of the friends that surrounded me.

My friends—near and far, lifelong and new—I love you all. I collectively thank you for handling my quirks with grace and love.

## A Word on Grief

Chances are you have lost a person you loved, or you know someone who has, or you are about to. One time I called my former college roommate Sheri at eleven at night, because each time I tried to sleep, my thoughts went to Deb: memories of her, memories of how she died, torturous thoughts of her terrifying last moments. I called Sheri because she had told me I could call anytime. While she was able to attend Deb's funeral, she expressed her concern about not being able to help me long-term for two reasons: distance and wisdom.

What can you do about distance? We live where we live. Even those many years ago, calling plans were "all inclusive." There were no worries about exorbitant long-distance charges, so phone calls were accessible. The bigger issue was wisdom. Sheri expressed to me in one of our conversations that she felt clueless as to how to support me. The general sense of my reply was to ask. Ask me about Deb. Ask me what keeps me up at night. Ask me what feels heavy.

Isolation is easy—too easy—when you are in shock and grieving. My thoughts were a revolving door from "no one cares" to "don't label me." The tricky side of isolation is that I didn't know I was isolating myself. Or maybe I did, a bit, which is why on occasion, when I was desperate, I would reach out to a friend like Sheri. It was so nice of her to answer her phone and stay on with me for quite a while. Knowing myself, I am sure we spent more time catching up on life than talking about what was causing my sleeplessness but her friendly voice helped.

I share this to introduce a difficult subject: grief support. This American theory of pulling up your bootstraps and moving on by yourself is garbage. When you have lost part of your heart, life may never seem as colorful again. Mourning and grief takes time—years, even. And that person you love who is wading through the swampy waters of grief needs you. Support them.

Through my involvement with Team World Vision, I have met many compassionate leaders. Buddy Shuh openly shares his journey of grief to assist others through the Tears Foundation he and his wife founded. His daughter Bella died when she was just six months old. That was ten years ago, yet there is still raw, deep emotion when he speaks of her. Of course! Who would dare tell a dad to "move on"? Buddy shared with me a conversation regarding grief that he had with a Jewish woman. She explained that at a Jewish funeral it is difficult to distinguish the family from friends. A mother who has lost a child, for instance, will be vocal in her grief, but she won't be alone in it. Her family and friends will encircle her and join in her moaning. Mourning is a group effort. It is comforting to imagine being surrounded by others who are similarly grief stricken, perhaps simply out of compassion for you.

Be the one to initiate the group hug of mourning. Let your friend cry and moan. Hand her tissues and water. Rub her back. When the tears dry, sit silently by her when she has no words. When you see her, always ask.

A business associate, Laura, gave me a welcome gift one night when I joined her at a restaurant after a meeting. As I and another associate settled into our chairs, she simply asked, "How are things going without your sister?"

My initial thought was how courageous she was. It had been several months since Deb died, and none of my friends from this particular circle had even mentioned my loss. I understood, though; it's tough. What if you ask and cause an emotional breakdown? Perhaps they don't want to talk about it. It is simpler to ignore the situation rather than risk revealing an open wound that boxes us into a sterile life devoid of the natural desire to connect with others.

We all are going to lose important people in our lives. Let's get better at sharing that burden.

At the very least, send chocolate.

## Acknowledgments

Since writing was never a bucket list item for me, I was surprised to hear my husband telling friends the subject of my next book. I wasn't even sure I was going to write a follow-up to *shoo g-er*. Then readers of *shoo g-er* started asking me when I would write the next one. Hmm, maybe God did want me to continue telling my story. So, thanks to Dave's faith in me, my boys' patience, and God blanketing me with memories and inspiration, *Chök'lit* was completed.

Of course it was unorganized, unclear, and in some places repetitive when I sent it to a handful of friends who agreed to be test readers. Bev, Heather, Karen, Kari, Kim, and Victoria agreed to read through all the messiness in only five days and report back on how I could improve it. I appreciate your insight and frankness, ladies. Your comments ignited a fresh approach that immensely improved the final product.

My mom and brother-in-law agreed to share their memories about Deb to help me fill out our stories and keep them accurate. Mom lost her daughter and Clayton his wife. The fact that they were willing to open up the door of grief again means so much to me.

Every Child Deserves Clean Water

We are a community of people helping each other get to the finish line while changing lives around the world. Team World Vision runs so that children in Africa can have clean water and fullness of life.

www.teamworldvision.org

The Tears Foundation helps bereaved families honor the lives of their children by compassionately assisting bereaved parents with the financial expenses they face in making final arrangements for their precious babies.

www.thetearsfoundation.org

# Available Titles from Joanna Lynne Krenk

## *shoo g-er*

*shoo g-er* begins with the sudden death of Joanna's father. Her story continues with additional life-altering events, including high-risk pregnancies, her sister's murder, and health challenges. Death, celebration, life-altering changes, and a miracle combine to create a sweet journey of faith. Drizzled with humor and heartbreak, *shoo g-er* is sure to satisfy.

## *Endurance*

Every triathlete knows that endurance is the key to success. This weekly devotional builds stamina in your spiritual walk as you train for your physical race.

In this twenty-six-week tri-votion, each week begins with a motivational verse and thoughts to consider. The facing page provides space for reflection on the verse and to keep training notes.

Build your endurance to finish well, both physically and spiritually.

**ALL PROFITS FROM BOOK SALES ARE DONATED TO TEAM WORLD VISION**

ABOUT THE AUTHOR

Joanna Lynne Krenk is a nostalgic child of the seventies whose most fond memories are wrapped in the music and fashion of the eighties and nineties. Her two teen-aged boys are rightly embarrassed by her loud singing and dancing, in which her husband, Dave, gladly joins in.

Made in the USA
Middletown, DE
09 March 2016